"Because we as believers will soon see Jesus face-to-face, we need to live intentionally for Him. *Pursue the Intentional Life* has stimulated me to think and act more intentionally so I can serve Him with my best until He calls me Home."

—DAVID RAE, president, Cables and Kits; former president, Apple Canada

"No one is better qualified to write *Pursue the Intentional Life* than Jean Fleming. Her single-hearted quest of 'becoming the person God had in mind when He created me' is exemplified in her life and writings. Over the years, Jean has kept an Old Woman File, and it is out of her 'rumblings and stirrings' as she pondered life on earth that we have this rich compilation of profound insights and lessons learned. In her words, 'the book is a collection of mooring cables attaching me to my Anchor.' You will find strong mooring cables here to challenge and encourage your relationship with Christ no matter where you are in your journey with Him. Jean's underlying theme addresses the question 'What does it look like to live Christ to the very end?' Read this priceless book to discover the answer."

—CYNTHIA HEALD, author of the BECOMING A WOMAN OF . . . Bible study series and *Intimacy with God*

"This book is vintage Jean Fleming. Its message addresses my recent reflections about finishing well, maximizing spiritual fruitfulness, and living for the glory of God in the fourth quarter of life. The biblical wisdom Jean shares in these pages would be profitable for anyone, regardless of age, who fears spiritual drifting and wants to pursue an intentional life."

—DON WHITNEY, associate professor of biblical spirituality and senior associate dean, The Southern Baptist Theological Seminary; founder and president, The Center for Biblical Spirituality

"Jean is a gifted writer and a passionate lover of Jesus. Her artistry shows clearly in her compelling word pictures that remind us of the joy of living our lives to the fullest and for God's glory at any stage of life and even into old age. You will be blessed and spiritually energized as you follow Jean's journey of reflection that prepares you for the future."

—MARY WHITE, coauthor of *Unfinished*

"*Pursue the Intentional Life* deals with a critically important life principle that deserves much more literary attention. This book is not only timely but also succinct, biblical, well referenced, practical, and often profound. That Jean Fleming is such an unusually gifted author gives this book value not only for the ideas expressed but also for the expression of those ideas. These words will not wear out."

—RICHARD A. SWENSON, MD,
best-selling author of *Margin* and *The Overload Syndrome*

"Do you want a book that is not so much a teaching book as it is a searching, asking, walk-with-me book that encourages you to ponder your life? Then this book is for you! Like Jean, I celebrated my seventieth birthday this year. I loved reading *Pursue the Intentional Life* as an older woman but would also have delighted in it at age thirty. I highly recommend it to you and believe that these pages will encourage, motivate, and inspire you just like they did me!"

—LINDA DILLOW, author of *Calm My Anxious Heart*;
coauthor of *Passion Pursuit*

JEAN FLEMING

PURSUE
THE
INTENTIONAL
LIFE

"Teach us to number our days, that we may

gain a heart of wisdom." Psalm 90:12 (NIV)

A NavPress resource published in alliance
with Tyndale House Publishers, Inc.

NavPress is the publishing ministry of The Navigators, an international Christian organization and leader in personal spiritual development. NavPress is committed to helping people grow spiritually and enjoy lives of meaning and hope through personal and group resources that are biblically rooted, culturally relevant, and highly practical.

For more information, visit www.NavPress.com.

Library of Congress Cataloging-in-Publication Data

Fleming, Jean.
    Pursue the intentional life : teach us to number our days, that we may gain a heart of wisdom (Psalm 90:12) / Jean Fleming.
        pages cm
    Includes bibliographical references.
    ISBN 978-1-61291-097-0
1. Christian life. I. Title.
    BV4501.3.F583 2013
    248.4—dc23
                                    2013013137

For the generations that come from us —

to the glory of God

"The children of your servants will live in your presence;

their descendants will be established before you."

Psalm 102:28

Matt and Lashawna

Beth and Lyle

Graham and Yasuko

And our grandchildren

CONTENTS

FOREWORD

It is early March in Colorado when I meet with Jean Fleming for the first time. We're sitting at Backstreet Bagels near First and Townsend. She sketches a tree on a paper napkin, putting heart-shaped leaves on the branches and writing "CHRIST" down the trunk. I know this tree; it's the one she wrote about in chapter 3 of *Between Walden and the Whirlwind*. This is our first face-to-face meeting, but I first met Jean through her writings. Now fourteen years into motherhood, I keep returning to *A Mother's Heart* (where the applications go beyond parenting). I've been reading and studying the Bible daily for some time, but *Feeding Your Soul: A Quiet Time Handbook* still guides me. Her "Open-Heart Bible Study" (in *Discipleship Journal*'s online archives) is an article I routinely distribute in my Bible-study groups. And I could never adequately express how much *The Homesick Heart* deeply ministers to my own.

Back to the bagel shop. Jean is drawing leaves, and I notice that her hand shakes a little as she writes. Her hair is white. Her children are my age. She tells me she's turning sixty-seven next month. I look over my coffee at this woman, thirty-one and a half years my senior, and wonder, *Why does she seem so . . . young?*

The Jean Fleming I have come to know, now in her seventies, is not old. A vitality radiates from her countenance and posture. She always greets me with an exuberant "Hey!" With alert eyes and listening heart, Jean seems to catch everything: the hidden meaning in my words, the unspoken emotions in my spirit. Winsome, attentive, and energetic, she attracts people to Christ. She thinks strategically about ministry concerns with youthful fervor. If Jean were a tree, she would be "full of sap and very green" (Psalm 92:14, NASB).

If a woman like this writes a book originating in the questions "What kind of old woman am I becoming?" and "Lord, how do You want me to think about the rest of my life?" then I am certainly going to read it.

Pursue the Intentional Life has future as well as immediate practical impact. Though you'll find phrases like "old woman" and "ending wisely" and "fiftieth year in Christ" in the following pages, this book is not specifically for "old people." *Pursue the Intentional Life* is for you who want to see the big picture of your life and God's purposes. It is for you who don't want to revert to default or live a haphazard life on cruise control. It is for you who seek to live meaningfully and intentionally in the present while preparing well for the future. This book could be for the middle-aged parent facing transition or crisis, the elderly considering his last days, or the twentysomething excited about a full life ahead.

Essentially a private journal made public, each chapter lets us listen in on Jean's conversations with herself and with God. Though Jean is a gifted teacher, here she doesn't teach so much as invite. "Welcome," the front cover conveys. "Come in and see what the Lord is showing me."

A two-mile path loops around Jean's neighborhood. "Want to go for a walk?" she asks. She shows me her collection of heart-shaped rocks, each one found among the gravel in the driveway or around the house. She points out an enchanting, narrow wooded place by the path and tells me it reminds her of something out of Narnia. She says that herons nest in those trees. She abruptly stops our walk and conversation to grab my arm and say, "Look!" I then notice an owl flying silently over the big pond.

"Did you see it?" she asks.

Yes, Jean, I did.

This is not a teaching book that claims to have all the answers; it is a searching, asking, walk-with-me book that stimulates my own thinking and hunger for God. It keeps me on my toes to maintain a healthy melding of consistent patterns and Spirit-sensitive flexibility. These chapters have brought me from fear to courage, from timidity to enthusiasm, from fatigue to refreshment. In considering the rest of life, Jean imparts a sense of urgency without panic. Her alertness makes me alert too, and she draws my attention to truths from God's Word that I may not have noticed otherwise. I might have missed the heron's nest, the heart rocks in the gravel, the owl on silent wings.

I've found that reading this book is a lot like my friendship and discipleship with Jean. In these pages, I learn by watching and walking beside her as she follows her own path with Christ. Her wit is endearing, her spirit humble, and her intellect sharp. Often, the indirect and subtle parts are the ones that help me most powerfully. Her life is in the words, and she shares this life with me. Reading this book is like going with Jean on the two-mile loop.

Want to go for a walk?

Monica Sharman

ACKNOWLEDGMENTS

I'm blessed with friends who care and pray. Thank you for your part in this book:

- Monica Sharman, who knows this book well
- Molly Hoyle, who graciously did some advance reading and commenting
- My daughter, Beth, whose insights are always worth considering
- Tania Najjar, who persevered to track down some difficult attributions
- Don Simpson, my esteemed editor and friend
- Jim and Debbie Selland, for a timely generosity
- Friends who let me use their stories and experiences
- My small group and Bible-study friends
- Most of all, Roger

CHAPTER 1

TAKE A WALK WITH ME: ASKING TWO BIG QUESTIONS

It all started when I turned fifty. I considered that most likely I was at least at the halfway point in my life, a thought I found both sobering and thrilling. On a long walk among the uplifted red-rock formations in Garden of the Gods in Colorado Springs, I prayed about what kind of old woman I would become and how I should think about my remaining years. I didn't have any great aspirations for that walk; I just didn't want to back into whatever was left of the rest of my life.

I walked under the strong blue sky and bracing April air. The wind lifted my hair and rustled the paper I carried. I stopped and jotted thoughts and made that folded page the first entry in my "Old Woman File." At the time, I had no idea that I had defined a groove of thought that I can profitably build on, refine, and live in all the way to the grave.

For twenty years, I've fed that file. I've studied Bible passages, collected quotes, and hoarded odd pages, snippets of conversation, and insights from books I was reading—whatever held the slightest promise of stimulating my thinking on this topic—all the while holding up one idea after another to the Scriptures, pondering and praying.

My spiritual siftings that April day served a concern: I feared living my remaining years vaguely, merely drifting in the wake of those living unconsidered lives. I desired to move into the coming years with vigor and focus. Then, too, I feared becoming a pinched and grouchy old person. The truth is that, all things unchanged, the women we will be at seventy, eighty, and ninety are the women we are at forty and fifty—only distilled. Have you noticed that the flaws and weaknesses of a forty-year-old concentrate with age? A complainer at forty will, with much practice, engrave the response in his or her bones by seventy. Self-centeredness will intensify. Bitterness, allowed to take root and grow over decades, engulfs and consumes in advanced age. Anyone living a frittering existence at thirty will, apart from a serious course correction, end up frittering away an entire life. It is just as true that a person doesn't suddenly become a wise, kind, gracious, fruitful old person just by reaching, say, seventy years. Of course, it's not too late to grow and change (I take comfort in that), but, more important, it's never too soon to begin.

This journey has unearthed some surprises. A young woman, a pastor's wife from the East Coast, asked, "When I come next time, will you take me through your 'Old Woman File'?" Why was I surprised at a young woman's interest? It is never too soon to prepare for the rest of our lives. The truth is that everyone, regardless of age, is already setting patterns for the shape of his or her life. These patterns of thought and practice will either serve the glory and purposes of God or hinder them.

I suspect that the material in my "Old Woman File" will benefit the young reader most of all. Even though a young person may be only mildly motivated by the question "What kind of an old person am I becoming?" he or she will recognize the value of preparing for the future. The issues I'm pondering make a difference today, next week, and next year—and into whatever time remains. These topics and truths impact life with God now—our joy and usefulness to the body—as well as our entry into the Lord's presence at death.

This book is the tangible result of my rumblings and stirrings as I've pondered life on earth, life with an expiration date, and life eternal with Jesus in heaven. It is the material evidence of my longing and intention to live in Jesus, with Jesus, and for Jesus to the end of my life. After all these years, I still find two questions motivating and challenging; more, I see them as infinitely consequential: What kind of old woman will I become? How will I live the rest of my life?

It's certain that I'm heading into the rest of my life with greater prospect because of my years handling the material in my "Old Woman File." The colors are brighter and clearer, the range of possibility greater than it would have been. My anticipation and attentiveness are increased. My antennae are up. I'm on a steep learning curve. The questions and seed thoughts that tumbled in the dryer drum of my mind that windy April day still intrigue, motivate, and sometimes unsettle.

And isn't that a good place to be as I head into the rest of my life?

Father, dear Father, only You know how many days I have left on earth and what joys, opportunities, and challenges are ahead for me. I give myself to You again. Lord God, I want my remaining days to be days of ascent, days of learning You and knowing You better. Bless me and guard me for the day I make my final ascent into Your presence. Please don't leave me to myself.

CHAPTER 2

WHY I WROTE THIS BOOK, HOW I PLAN TO USE IT, AND HOW YOU MIGHT USE IT TOO

At some point along the way, I thought of putting the accumulating material from my "Old Woman File" into a little book for my own use. Ideas were plumping. Layers of thought sharpened in my mind and I considered how I might best preserve them. I hoped to organize the material for easy access and reference—something to return to over and over, something to build on for the rest of my life.

Some might ask, "Why do you need to put this into a book when you have the Bible? Couldn't you just return to the Bible as you face various life situations?"

Of course—and I will. But as I've worked through—pondered and prayed over—the pages in my file, I've sought to organize a body of "pre-thought" to return to in times of difficulty and transition, times when I feel spiritually disoriented, times when I need a word of encouragement, direction, or rebuke. I read recently that some Puritans did the same thing. In the preface to a book of Puritan prayers, Arthur Bennett wrote that many Puritans kept "a record of God's intimate dealings with their souls, not with an eye to publication, but, as in David Brainerd's case, to test their spiritual growth, and to encourage themselves by their re-perusal in times of low spiritual fervor."[1] Bennett said they often wrote their prayers into the text, something that I was doing as well. I see this book as a touchstone in my spiritual journey, a concrete point, a tangible record of my thinking so far from which to journey onward, something in black and white to revert to for realignment, a book to help me live my highest until the Lord calls me home. I long to see Christ's life formed in me. I want to become the person God had in mind when He created me. I yearn to touch the world for God's glory and advance His kingdom. The substance of this book represents my earnest desire to "number [my] days . . . that [I] may gain a heart of wisdom" (Psalm 90:12).

My own longings, questions, fears—and the glories I'm probing—spur me on. I don't know what the future holds. Will I be a widow? Face serious illness? Know loneliness and isolation? Much of what is ahead is unknown, but the known part is meat and bread for the soul. The known part, what God has revealed through His Word, is food for the journey, whatever my age, whatever twists and dips life takes. Food for the journey—maybe that's a good way to express my hope for this book. I believe that God wants me to feed on His Word and be shaped by it, to take His promises, warnings, and instructions seriously. I believe He wants me to tune in. Tuning in may be my best preparation for living the rest of my life well. I pray that you may be enriched spiritually as well.

Preparation is an important concept in the Bible. Throughout the Gospels and especially just before His passion (see John 13–16), Jesus prepares His disciples for the horrors of His death, the shock waves of His resurrection, and the years of ministry ahead. Much of what He said jelled for them only after the Holy Spirit came, but the dense content of His teaching instructed, reminded, and motivated them for the rest of their lives. When grief, confusion, and doubt assaulted the disciples, Jesus' words flowered in their minds. He delivered a fabric of teaching to prepare His followers so they were neither immobilized nor stampeded. Just as He made preparations for the care of His mother, He planned ahead for the care of His disciples, leaving them—and us—a rich body of truth.

The Scriptures contain what I will need when the wind whips the waves and sets them towering above me. Like Peter in the squall, I may falter, but, also like Peter, I can be stirred to faith (see Matthew 14:22-33). I can be called higher. In that regard, I see my book as a collection of mooring cables attaching me to my Anchor, a resource for times when I need to batten down the hatches or turn and face the wind. I view my work on this book as my preparation for the years left to me.

I've included Scripture and, where the Scripture isn't printed, the reference. Over these next years, as I seek to deepen my understanding of these topics, I will return to these Bible passages to ponder and pray. As you read the chapters, you will profit most if you do the same. Likewise, if my prayers express your desire, pray them along with me. If not, shape prayers that give voice to God's moving in your own life.

Food Ready to Eat: A Prepared Meal

I think of Elijah in his "storm" fleeing Queen Jezebel's evil wrath. He was afraid, exhausted, depressed, and despairing. This courageous but depleted servant of God sat under a broom tree and prayed to die (see 1 Kings 19:4). Elijah was a man of faith who had just defeated 450 prophets of Baal in a spiritual duel. Now he was running for his life. He knew God, he knew the Scriptures, but in his exhausted state, he needed nourishment provided by another. An angel wakes and feeds him, twice. Elijah wakes to the aroma of warm bread ready for consumption. Because Elijah was neither physically nor emotionally capable of fixing himself a meal, God sent an angel-cook.

> Lord, I know there are times when I need some already-baked bread. Maybe in storms or times of depletion, confusion, or disappointment, I need the fragrant aroma of food still on the coals. Help me to put this book together that it might feed me in times of exhaustion, fear, and uncertainty.

A Stewardship of Insights to Return To

I most often hear the word *stewardship* used in regards to money, talents, and time. My husband reminds me to be a good steward of the insights God gives as well. Revelations are graces from God not to be received lightly. For me, that means setting down on paper thoughts that might evaporate if left floating in the air. The ideas I explore, pray over, and chew on form a body of truth-in-process for me. I catch glimmers, fully intending to watch over them like a hen over her hatch. I return to these forming ideas, asking the Lord to correct, enlarge, and refine them. I compile and organize the fruit of my "Old Woman File" into a book of my own as a stewardship. This book is my attempt to honor revelation that I might preserve and return to it.

A Rock of Respite

This book is a rock in a turbulent stream. It is a higher place in a world of trouble. When life swirls and buffets, I pull myself out of the choking current onto my rock. I open my book and trust the Lord to build on what He's shown me so far. I pause for Him to remind me of realities I lose sight of in the tempest. From this elevation, I gain a fresh perspective. I catch my breath. In the restoring lull, I sense His breath igniting my spirit again to trust Him. And with renewed faith, I slip back into the waters ordained for me.

An Inspiration to Vision and Courage

Transitions always come with endings: the end of a job, the end of a marriage, the end of a dream, the end of robust health. When something ends, there is the possibility of new beginnings. Nevertheless, most endings feel like the end, a time of heavy cloud cover. With that realization, I envision my book as a ready, available reminder that God is the God of my endings and beginnings. Here, in the presence of God, I acknowledge my loss and ask for direction, courage, and faithfulness in the new and undefined future.

Putting Life into the Greater Context

Novelist Katherine Anne Porter wrote, "Human life itself may be almost pure chaos, but the work of the artist—the only thing he's good for—is to take these handfuls of confusion and disparate things, things that seem to be irreconcilable, and put them together in a frame to give them some kind of shape and meaning."[2] Certainly, there is complexity and mystery to life on earth, but not chaos. The sovereign God is executing His purposes and plans. He is neither impotent nor capricious. All things are moving to a sure, ordered, and ordained end. The wonder is that He has revealed much of His intent, even giving glimpses into the very hearth of heaven. So, with the wide-screen view of earth and heaven in mind, I (like David Brainerd) write a book for my own use. I hope it will be illuminating for you, my reader, as well.

> Sovereign God, holy and good, righteous and gracious, God of the macro and the micro, meet with me in my attempt to capture something of what You show me. By Your grace and mercy, give me a repenting and pliable heart and mind. Teach me. Train me. Refine me. Renew me. Bless me that I might be a blessing. Use my work on this book to capture my heart and the heart of my reader, more and more, now and to the end, for Jesus' sake.

CHAPTER 3

RESOLUTION 52: COMMITMENT TO A REFLECTIVE LIFE

Resolution 52: "I frequently hear persons in old age say how they would live, if they were to live their lives over again: Resolved, that I will live . . . as . . . I shall wish I had done, supposing I live to old age."

JONATHAN EDWARDS

Jonathan Edwards (1703–1758) had seventy resolutions, all written when he was in his early twenties. If he'd had an editor, the number would have been, perhaps, thirty resolutions because many sound so similar, but to his careful and disciplined mind, each brought a shade of meaning that required distinct pondering. For example, Resolution 50 says, "Resolved, I will act so as I think I shall judge would have been best, and most prudent, when I come into the future world."[1] Edwards projects. He imagines. When he stands on heaven's shores and looks back over his shoulder, how will he evaluate his life on earth? How will his life, now ended, appear to him? Edwards doesn't wait until it is too late to change things; he considers the question while still a young man so that he can finish his course in joy, not sorrow and shame.

In Resolution 52, Edwards imagines himself as an older man and probes the question "If I were living my life over, what changes would I make?" While still a young man, Edwards runs the reel fast-forward. He slowly backs up and scrutinizes possible future choices and decisions. He scans for character fault lines, seams and cracks that cause a life to shatter or crumble. He determines to follow God and His ways all his life.

Resolution 7: "Resolved, never to do anything, which I should be afraid to do, if it were the last hour of my life."

Resolution 17: "Resolved, that I will live so as I shall wish I had done when I come to die."

Resolution 18: "Resolved, to live so at all times, as I think is best in my devout frames, and when I have clearest notions of things of the gospel, and another world."

What do I take away from these resolves? Jonathan Edwards's resolves remind me (and warn me) that I will not live wisely or well if I just barrel (or shuffle) thoughtlessly through life. An unexamined life surely leads to unnecessary regrets, especially at the end of life. Although I don't plan to assemble seventy resolutions for myself, Edwards' vigorous determination to live thoughtfully and intentionally inspires me.

Edwards was a good husband, father, and pastor. Some consider him the greatest intellect North America produced. He was a scholar, theologian, university president, and missionary who was influential in the Great Awakening. He was, also, a master of reflection. Edwards read his seventy resolutions each week. That kind of reflection requires time. That time requires choosing and pruning. In the frantic pace of life, where do I find the time to reflect? I don't find it; I work at reserving and preserving it, just like Edwards did.

Lord God, soon I will be in Your presence with nothing between us. All this world's aberrations vanished, only the clear air of heaven between us. On that day of grace and glory, I know I will have regrets. I will wish for do-overs, wish I could go back to live more fervently for You. The reality is, I have only today and whatever tomorrows You've ordained for me.

I want to *be* Your person and *do* Your will. To that end, develop in me a reflective bent. Raise questions that lead to fruitful pondering. Attune my spirit to Your Spirit. Awaken drowsy parts of me. Stir me to trust You in all things. Enable me to discern good from evil and to choose the good. Help me live each day with the future in mind, that future day when I see You, whom I love without seeing.

This chapter is deliberately short. It reminds me that I need not fill every space. Instead, I must cultivate a leanness that leaves room for reflection.

CHAPTER 4

A PREPARED LIFE: THE ART OF ADVANCE-WORK TOWARD AN END

Some years ago, while scanning the shelves at the library, I saw an intriguing title: *The Fine Art of Recuperation.*[1] Although I didn't pull that book down and read it, the title alone aroused my interest. Although I haven't had occasion for medical recuperation since noticing that title, I think my attitude and approach toward a time of enforced inactivity due to recovering from surgery or a broken bone would be markedly different because of the thought that title inspired. Instead of dreading the span of "dead space," marking time, healing an incision or a femur, I would seek to learn something of the art of recuperation, the art of drawing the blankets around me to know God in deeper ways.

There is something about looking ahead, pondering a circumstance of life (recuperation, financial stress, child rearing, widowhood) to know something of the mind of God, and reminding myself of His promises that readies me for the future. This attitude may be one thing I have in common with the great Roman orator Marcus Tullius Cicero, who died in 43 BC. Cicero wrote about aging and said that "the composition of [his] book has been so delightful that it has not only wiped away all the disagreeables of old age, but has even made it luxurious and delightful too."[2] Maybe Cicero is given to hyperbole, but I think he makes a good point: Concentrated thought on an aspect of life can infuse it with meaning and possibilities. This is especially true when I give thought to the rest of my life.

I'm taken with the frequency of the word *prepare* in the Old and New Testaments. To prepare is to do advance-work toward an end. Embedded in Jesus' injunction to "watch and pray" is a call to spiritual preparation *now* for what one may face in the future. Solomon evidently agrees. He repeats his warning to look ahead and make adjustments: "The prudent see danger and take refuge, but the simple keep going and pay the penalty" (Proverbs 27:12; see also 22:3).

As I think about my remaining years, about possible challenges and opportunities, I make *mind* and *spirit* preparations. Desiring to face what comes in His strength to His glory, I set pegs and drive stakes. I ponder His Person and truth. I wonder, *What choices made today will enable me to finish my course with spiritual vigor? Is preparation key to the art of living Christ to the end?*

Not that I expect to sail through hard times untouched. But I trust God that my advance-work will give me a body of content to return to in challenging times, content to draw me to God, His promises, and His purposes.

Louis Pasteur said that chance favors a prepared mind.[3] It was true for Arturo Toscanini (1867–1957), the world acclaimed conductor. At nineteen, Toscanini, a cellist, had memorized the music for each instrument in the orchestra. His extraordinary preparation opened the door to a conducting career. After a series of occurrences during a performance in Rio de Janeiro, the young Toscanini stepped up and, without a score, led the orchestra. Similarly, Florence Nightingale, in a family and culture hostile to women pursuing a career in nursing, set herself to learning everything she could about nursing and hospital management. Hours of personal study and seeking out those most knowledgeable in the field and years of discouragement when all her preparation seemed in vain finally climaxed during the Crimean War when she was asked to set up a hospital for wounded soldiers in Turkey. Her preparation made her the leading authority on nursing best practice and hospital management.

Preparation makes a difference. Those who prepare for job interviews by writing out possible questions and answers do better than those who don't prepare. Air travelers who count the rows to the exits, study how to open emergency exit doors, and don't wear synthetic fabrics that meld to skin in a fire are more likely to survive an airplane crash. The list goes on. Pasteur is right: Chance favors a prepared mind.

Does looking ahead to prepare go against Jesus' words to give no thought to tomorrow (see Matthew 6:34)? The context makes it clear: Jesus warns against *worrying* about tomorrow, not about *preparing* for tomorrow. Laelius, a contemporary of Cicero, understood the benefits of advance preparation for aging. He asked Cicero to "allow us to learn from [him] in good time before it arrives, by what methods we may most easily acquire the strength to support the burden of advancing age."[4]

Katharine Graham, formerly publisher of the *The Washington Post*, speaking about the challenges of aging, said, "The second issue we have to face is what to do with our time. You have to be involved in something that makes you want to spring out of bed in the morning. This doesn't happen automatically. You have to plan for it. Paradoxically, you can't face old age when you're old. You have to face it when you're young."[5]

I'm not primarily concerned with issues of aging; I just want to honor the Lord and be a blessing until the end of my life. So I ask questions: What does it look like to live a beautiful life in a fallen world?

How can I prepare my heart and mind for the challenges, opportunities, and transitions that will come? What does it look like to live Christ to the very end?

> As I look ahead, Lord, reveal Yourself more fully to me. Teach me how to prepare for the rest of my life. What issues do I need to consider? What truths must grip me more completely? Lead me as I seek to make responsible preparations in my mind, heart, and will. May my preparations be informed and fortified with the great hope of the faith.

Mark Buchanan wrote, "The heart in fall is, in a word, expectant. If we've prepared well in spring, plowing and sowing and planting, then we wait in expectancy of hope. If we have not prepared well, we wait in an expectation of disappointment, maybe dread."[6]

Spring is the best time for planting if I want a good harvest in the fall. Vision, values, character, and disciplines developed in the springtime of life serve even into winter. Whatever the age, it is not too soon to prepare for the rest of life. Looking ahead, giving thought, pondering what I know of God, His will and ways, taking appropriate actions as a result, strengthens me rather than fosters dread. Thinking about my death, old age, and the possible challenges I may face stirs my desire to trust God, whatever comes. Even contemplating hard things, things that may or may not happen, prompts me to ask, "Lord, what content, what truth, what promises might help me to trust You and live for Your glory in this circumstance?"

Preparation sparks enthusiasms as well as quiet trust. As I dwell on God's Person and promises, I am strengthened for the unknown future. I remember that terror and dread are often curses on those who refuse to call on God. "But there they are, overwhelmed with dread, where there was nothing to dread" (Psalm 53:5). God brought terror on the disobedient, but His blessing is freedom from terror: "You will not fear the terror of night" (91:5). I prepare and trust in His promised blessing on His own children. Perhaps this is the art of living the rest of my life well.

Father, You are a God of preparation. You prepared a garden for the first family and a fish to swallow Jonah, and You are preparing a place in heaven for us. You called Noah to prepare an ark and the slaves in Egypt to prepare the first Passover feast. Now guide me by Your Spirit to make wise preparation as well. By Your grace and mercy, lead me that I might finish my life on earth trusting and growing in You. Draw me into sweet communion, a fuller knowledge and experience of You as You really are. Whatever the future holds, please keep me from terror and bless me to live for Your glory and the advancement of Your kingdom.

CHAPTER 5

MY INTENDED WING: RESOLVING AN INNER CONFLICT

April 2009 marked my fiftieth year in Christ. I was deeply moved when I realized I had gone fifty years in the same direction and would unequivocally choose the same direction for the next fifty. I wept in gratitude and thought again of my father's comment: "With Jean, nothing lasts more than three weeks." It was true. Before Christ claimed me, I flitted from one philosophical strain to the next, unsatisfied. So, after fifty years, I glory in God's keeping power, His great kindness and faithfulness. I look back over my life and shudder at the multitude of crossroads where the Lord intervened and answered my prayer, "Please don't leave me to myself."

My "Old Woman File" project really grew out of desire and fear. I ache to walk with the Lord to the very end, to bring Him glory; that is the sunshine. I fear dishonoring the Lord; that is the shadow. The sunshine and shadow met for me in the verse I chose for the year, a verse to live in and pray over again and again.

Verse for the Year 2009

I think I was attracted to Philippians 1:20 because the apostle Paul wasn't afraid of ending poorly. He was roughly sixty years old when he wrote, "For I live in eager expectation and hope that I will never do anything that will cause me to be ashamed of myself but that I will always be ready to speak out boldly for Christ while I am going through all these trials here, just as I have in the past; and that I will always be an honor to Christ, whether I live or whether I must die" (TLB).

The phrase "I live in eager expectation and hope" conjured up a picture that I sketched in my journal, a stick man in a cloud of eager expectation. The picture of *living in* an atmosphere of eager expectation and hope dispelled anxiety and replaced it with a light and soaring wing. Paul's life was like that; all around Paul hung an atmosphere of eager expectation and hope. When Paul entered a room, the weather changed. When he walked in, he brought an electrical current suffused with expectation and hope.

Every life creates an atmosphere. The air around some people is charged with rage. The air crackles, stretched taut, waiting for the lightning strike. Another person, another atmosphere: anxiety and tension, or fearfulness and excessive caution, or recklessness and indifference.

"I live in eager expectation and hope." What would it be like to live *in* an atmosphere of earnestness and exhilaration? Of enthusiasm and gameness? Of anticipation and readiness? What atmosphere will color the rest of my life? Will I live in eager expectation and hope or *in* something else—in apathy, in fear, in confusion, in anxiety, in hesitancy, in dread? Will my life be empowered and set aglow by unfading hope or drained away by parasites?

Eager Expectation and Hope

Eager is such a spirited word, full of energy and expectation. Eager speaks to me of moving into the rest of my life with anticipation and open arms rather than cringing in hesitation and fear.

Lord, I want to advance toward whatever You have ordained
for me between now and death with a light and eager spirit.
My hope is in You. Even if I walk in the dark and have no light,
grace me to trust in Your name and rely on You, as we're told
in Isaiah 50:10.

This can be my time of greatest growth in Christ, the final stretch
to the finish line, a time to put away every stale and self-protective
barrier and make a dash for the tape. My best years, my richest insights,
a time of quiet fruitfulness, various and ripe—my deepest experiences
of Christ are still ahead of me. This is my eager expectation. This is my
time of ripened fruit and flight, living increasingly in the reality of the
resurrection life, my heart and mind set on things above, earnest and
ready, expectant and alert.

The word for *expectation* that Paul uses in Philippians 1:20 is
found in only one other place in the Bible, Romans 8:19: "For the
creation waits in eager expectation for the children of God to be
revealed." In *Word Pictures in the New Testament*, Robertson quotes
Milligan's rendering: "to watch eagerly with outstretched head."[1] Yes,
head—perhaps like a man standing on the train platform eagerly
waiting, leaning forward as he watches for its arrival.

Struggling with *Always* and *Never*

As much as I loved that first phrase, "I live in eager expectation and
hope," in *The Living Bible*, I decided to memorize the verse in the
New International Version, the translation I use every day: "I eagerly
expect and hope that I will in no way be ashamed, but will have sufficient courage so that now as always Christ will be exalted in my body,
whether by life or by death." I wanted to make the verse my own but
felt uncomfortable with Paul's use of *always* and *never* in *The Living
Bible*. How could Paul, not knowing the future, put in black and
white that he would *never* do anything that would cause him shame,

that he would *always* be bold for Christ, and that his life would *always* honor Christ? I balked. Using *never* and *always* seemed presumptuous, cocky, and disingenuous. I expected better from the great apostle of the faith.

Then it hit me: Paul was expressing his "intended wing." That phrase, "intended wing," comes from a poem by John Milton:

Unless an age too late, or cold
Climate, or years, damp my intended wing.[2]

These lines from Milton's poem capture a reality. I have high intentions, aspirations to know God and honor Him, but so many things can dampen and dilute holy hungers. Life on earth has a way of smothering high intention, of curtailing flight, of dampening spiritual heat.

Like me, Paul doesn't know the ins and outs of the rest of his life. "Always" the future holds unknowns. We "never" know everything about the rest of our lives. Paul opens his heart to us. The apostle bares to us his intended wing. He intends that he will always be bold for Christ and will never live to cause shame. In the same chapter of this letter, Paul reminds the believers in Philippi (and us) that it is God who works in them to will and do His good pleasure (see Philippians 2:13). Like Paul, I can express my intended wing because it doesn't all depend on me; God is at work in me to bring me through to the end.

God implants this high desire to know and serve Him in His children. I see it in Paul and I see it in Jonathan Edwards, the early American pastor who compiled seventy resolutions for his life. He called his high intentions resolutions. I've chosen to call them intentions for two reasons. One, I have many failed resolutions. Two, although the words are closely related, in my mind, the word *resolutions* calls more to my flesh. Resolution conjures up spikes, an ice ax, and a jutted jaw. Whereas intentions or intended wing feels like a desperate surrender, trusting the Lord to undertake for me, the goal is still the high places, but the gear feels lighter—lighter, but still requiring an avid will.

Inherent in my intended wing is my acknowledged inadequacy and my high desire. The years ahead are my journey of learning and failing and learning. But in the process, my goal is that what I learn and what I say will become more and more a reality in my mind of minds, heart of hearts, and every action.

Sufficient Courage

Paul speaks of "sufficient courage." Sufficient courage for what? Enough courage to live in such a way that Christ will be exalted in his body, whether by life or by death. The word *courage* (NIV) or *boldness* (NASB) is *parrhesia* in the Greek. My commentary indicates two meanings: one, forthrightness in public speaking, freedom in speaking; two, free and fearless confidence, cheerful courage, boldness and courage.[3]

> Father God, please grace me with courage. I want to grow in
> bold proclamation of the gospel, fearlessly and confidently
> speaking eternal truths. I want to live to the very end with a
> cheerful courage, trusting You to uphold me and carry me
> through to my last breath. None of this is possible apart from
> Your empowering and sustaining grace. Please don't leave me
> to myself.

Just as Paul spoke of Christ unflinchingly in dungeon dankness, while others might have cowered in despair, so a person well along in years who speaks with assurance of Christ is a warm light in a cold world. When Christ loses no luster though a disciple's strength declines, when the gospel powerfully manifests itself through weakened flesh, when the Word of God surges unimpeded from frailty, Christ is exalted in that body.

The subject of courage came up recently in a conversation at church. A woman mentioned the courage of older women who often in pain get up, dress up, and come to church. Just to keep going in old age can require enormous courage. The same can be said for men who work to support their families in a job they don't like, looking to God for the greater reward; or women, weary and stretched, who cheerfully get children off to school morning after morning strengthened by the joy of the Lord; or that housebound woman or man who could succumb to self-pity but instead supports others in prayer.

It is my intention, my intended wing, to live with cheerful courage. Like Paul, I want to live buoyed by Christ's life in me, full of eager expectation and hope. Perhaps that is a good picture of surrender: to float in Christ. Floating in Christ is not passivity or limp-muscled resignation; Paul puts forth plenty of effort. The verbs Paul employs in this letter to the Philippians vibrate with tension and strain: "press on," "take hold," and "straining toward." Pressing and floating, Paul releases concern over failing Christ, trusting Christ to hold him up. Paul is fully and energetically engaged, but he puts "no confidence in the flesh" (3:3). His body, mind, and spirit are in gear. The greatest commandment requires it: "Love the Lord your God with all your heart and with all your soul and with all your mind" (Matthew 22:37).

I take courage, Lord. My intended wing is to bring You glory. I know that nobody soars all the time, but I trust You to keep me to the end.

CHAPTER 6

NOBODY SOARS ALL THE TIME: DE-ROMANTICIZING THE LIFE OF FAITH

On my walk today, I stop to watch a red-tailed hawk flap and soar over Mexican Gulch. Captivated, I hold his seemingly effortless current-riding in my gaze until he disappears. I want to soar. I think about my intended wing — my life of intention — and about the challenges I might face in the future. I can't imagine "soaring" if I lost my husband. And I wonder, *Was Jesus soaring in Gethsemane when He sweat great drops of blood? Was He soaring when He agonized in prayer, repeatedly pleading for another path? Was Paul soaring when he despaired of life, when he and his coworkers hit the limit of what they felt they could endure?* "We were under great pressure, far beyond our ability to endure, so that we despaired of life itself. Indeed, we felt we had received the sentence of death" (2 Corinthians 1:8-9). Was David soaring when, in fear, he pretended to be insane (see 1 Samuel 21:12-13)? Can a man be soaring as he slobbers on his beard?

I want to soar, but I struggle to define what I mean by soaring. It is an unexpected conflict. It seems only right that those emancipated from sin's stranglehold (see Romans 6:18) — redeemed from the weight of guilt and shame, given a new name and nature, and promised an inheritance that can never perish, spoil, or fade — should live with airborne spirits. I believe that the desire to soar is God-given, but the idea of soaring moves me dangerously toward idealizing the Christian life. A romanticized view of life in Christ is destructive, not to mention dishonoring to God. If soaring conjures up pictures of living above life's circumstances, untouched by grief, discouragement, fear, and pain, then I've romanticized — and perverted — God's intention.

I notice that the Bible gives a decidedly unromantic picture of life on earth. God doesn't censor the soul-raw moments of His best men. He refuses to airbrush fear, despair, failure, and discouragement. I wonder if He includes these spiritually X-rated parts to deflower my distorted picture of what it means to walk with Him.

It's true that wings give us the capacity to preside over a larger view of life. From the heights, I gain perspective. Whether the brutal occurrence or the draining mundane, I'm blessed when, by grace, God allows me to ride the currents of greater truths. Unlike someone seated in a deep hole, seeing only that square of sky directly above, a soarer, set in a flight pattern of God's great gospel truths, has the advantage of an enlarged view, even if stumbling along.

My Emotions Are Not a Reliable Gauge of My Spiritual Condition

Perhaps one reason I love Psalms is that David is so real, so honest, so human. His emotional upheavals push through dry crust like molten lava. David is all heat and flow. His prayers come from the heart, uncensored. He wrote,

My heart is in anguish within me;
    the terrors of death have fallen on me.
Fear and trembling have beset me;
    horror has overwhelmed me.
I said, "Oh, that I had the wings of a dove!
    I would fly away and be at rest.
I would flee far away
    and stay in the desert;
I would hurry to my place of shelter,
    far from the tempest and storm." (55:4-8)

He ended the psalm, "But as for me, I trust in you" (verse 23). His erupting emotions subsided. Though the circumstance remained unchanged, David placed himself, perhaps still anguished and fearful, in the hands of God. His emotions were not a reliable gauge of his spiritual condition. Though David sometimes stumbled and slobbered along, he soared, too. Perhaps the distance between stumbling and soaring is not so great after all.

I read the Bible and remind myself that God made humans *human* and said, "It is good." Even before sin, Adam and Eve were not super-human. Their naked perfection reflected their inner nakedness and need. By design, humans are not self-sufficient. Adam and Eve were created to walk with God, enjoy Him, obey Him, and find their supply in God Himself. When Paul and his coworkers tottered on the brink, he concluded, "This happened that we might not rely on ourselves but on God, who raises the dead" (2 Corinthians 1:9). They come to the utter end of themselves, surrender themselves to God and experience His resurrection power, and they soar.

Ironically, to soar I must taste my weakness and need. In the turbulence of life, I reach out to God. Surely, hurricane gales would carry me off if God's firm grip failed. But His love will not let me go. I find refuge in Him, and I soar. I soar in the growing knowledge and experience of God Himself. He reveals Himself in Word as faithful, compassionate, loving, and able. The Lord meets me in my "squall." Life's storms and stresses draw me closer to Him. I soar most in the shadow of *His* wings (see Psalm 91:1-2,4).

Soaring and Stumbling

Years ago, our family flew back from an assignment in Asia on a flight that island-hopped across the South Pacific. We landed on one island little longer than the runway. On another island, we walked with our toddlers amidst ground-nesting albatross. Albatross, long-winged majestic seabirds best known from Coleridge's epic poem *The Rime of the Ancient Mariner*, spend eighteen months at sea, touching down only on water, losing their ability to make smooth earth-landings. Returning to nest and lay eggs, they come in like drunken sailors, tumbling, skidding, crashing, earning these regal birds the epithet *gooney birds*.

These powerful seabirds spread enormous wings, sometimes reaching an eleven-foot span, and glide above turbulent seas. They need storm-strong wind currents to keep them aloft. In calm seas, they are virtually unable to get airborne. The doldrums, a band of calm, prevent albatross migration from the Southern Hemisphere. Storms will come for me, too. I need them. My intended wing, my high desire for God, will be tested and developed in strong winds and troubled waters. I eagerly expect and hope that God will enable me to ride the turbulence and learn the currents of grace. Riding on currents of grace doesn't preclude stumbles, skids, or nosedives.

Unfortunately, pockets of thought untouched by gospel-grace remain. Old thought-action patterns hinder. Maybe my stumbling, tumbling times train me in sustaining grace. God knows I need the grace-thermals. Though I want to soar, maybe God will make me, like the albatross, fruitful even after a crash landing.

Isn't that like Him? Isn't that grace?

Perhaps the desire to soar comes with the new birth. I'm more than a "mere human"; like the albatross, which reproduce after a rough landing, I am a new creation (see 2 Corinthians 5:17). The Holy Spirit lives in me (see 1 Corinthians 3:16). I am no longer a slave to sin (see Romans 6:18). God gives His very great and precious promises so I may live life on a higher plane (see 2 Peter 1:3-4). I aspire to live more fully in the resources of my new life in Christ.

Yet God knows that I will not always soar:

> He gives strength to the weary
>> and increases the power of the weak.
> Even youths grow tired and weary,
>> and young men stumble and fall;
> but those who hope in the Lord
>> will renew their strength.
> They will soar on wings like eagles;
>> they will run and not grow weary,
>> they will walk and not be faint. (Isaiah 40:29-31)

I will know times of soaring, times of running, times of walking, and times of stumbling, but in Him, my strength is renewed, my faltering step steadied, my gaze lifted above the tangled brush of life to see again my God, my hope. Who knows the assortment of challenges ahead? But in them all, I want to trust His grace, trust that He can reveal Himself in me even when I'm barely hanging on, trust that when there is almost nothing of me left, He will show up most powerfully (see 2 Corinthians 12:9).

Father God, please keep me from distorted ideas of what it means to walk with You. In my deep desire to live on the heights, keep me from romanticizing what that looks like. At this point, I think soaring is trusting that You can glorify Yourself through me no matter what. The only limiting factor is me, and, glory of glories, You can use me in spite of myself, just as You have used other frail, flailing failures such as Jonah, Gideon, Peter, and every other human You used through the ages. Grace, grace, amazing grace.

When hard times come — confusing times, faltering times — encircle me with Your protecting, sustaining care. Remember my intended wing and catch me up again on the strong currents of Your mercy and grace — Your faithfulness, not mine, Your life in me. You know my weak humanity, and it's not a problem to You. You prefer me weak and trusting so Your grace might be unfettered. Praise upon praise to Your Holy Name.

CHAPTER 7

TEACH US TO NUMBER OUR DAYS: THE MINISTRY OF THE OBITUARY

Teach us to number our days, that we may gain a heart of wisdom.

PSALM 90:12

I was pondering Psalm 90:12 when I read this humorous paragraph from a novel by contemporary American writer Don DeLillo. He wrote, "When I read obituaries I always note the age of the deceased. Automatically I relate this figure to my own age. Four years to go, I think. Nine more years. Two years and I'm dead. The power of numbers is never more evident than when we use them to speculate on the time of our dying."[1]

Was the character from the novel morbid? Or maybe insightful? I think he's right. Of course I don't know the number of my days; I don't know if tomorrow will be my last day, but every year I pass—unheralded—the anniversary of my death.

Numbering my days isn't about computing days but rather about drawing me to attentiveness. Life on earth is a brief sojourn — brief but not unimportant, brief but not inconsequential. Numbering my days draws me up short and gives me an opportunity to resist the inclination to drift thoughtlessly. I use it as an excuse for arithmetic. The exercise has value. Where do I start? Moses wrote, "Our days may come to seventy years, or eighty, if our strength endures" (Psalm 90:10). How many days until I reach seventy? Today I multiply 365 days times 2 (years) plus the number of days until my birthday. The number comes to almost 800 days. Eight hundred days. A lot can happen in eight hundred days.

> Father, I don't know how many days I have left, but if I live another eight hundred days, how do You want me to think about them? How do You want me to use them? Jesus lived only thirty-three years. The number of days isn't restrictive. Many days or few, please teach me to live them wisely, connected to You.

I find that contemplating the end of life leads not to depression but to clarity and invigoration. Setting my life in parentheses and holding it at arm's length helps me to think more critically about the direction of my life. I once asked the Lord, "If I had only one year left to live, what would be my best contribution to our church?" That question led me to gather six young moms around my dining room table twice a month for Bible study, prayer, and personal mentoring. Similar questions are good to ask: "What would be most important to our family? If I had only one year to live, how should I order my days?"

Numbering my days forces me to confront universal and irreducible truths. Life is short. Soon my life on earth will give way to my life in heaven. Rather than leading to panic, the reality leads to a peaceful and settled urgency. Although thoughts of heaven are so lovely to consider, the Lord reminds me that my short stay on earth is my only chance to honor Him with faith and faithfulness. Isn't this, after all, gaining a heart of wisdom?

> Show me, Lord, my life's end
>> and the number of my days;
>> let me know how fleeting my life is.
> You have made my days a mere handbreadth;
>> the span of my years is as nothing before you.
>> Everyone is but a breath, even those who seem secure.
> Surely everyone goes around like a mere phantom;
>> in vain they rush about, heaping up wealth without
>> knowing whose it will finally be. (Psalm 39:4-6)

Speed Lines

Former poet laureate Billy Collins wrote a poem called Velocity.[2] From a speeding railway car on the way to Omaha, the poet, facing the blank page, draws the face of a motorcyclist in profile, thinning hair streaming behind, with speed lines drawn in. Collins remembers college theologians insisting that we must look at things from the perspective of eternity and thinks that we all must have speed lines flowing from us, even as we sleep.

He's right. We're all pushed from the birth canal trailing speed lines, and they will accompany us our entire journey. Even the loneliest person, housebound and bedridden, whose life seems to drag on — interminably, drably — has speed lines streaming from him or her. The Bible speaks of the speed lines poetically: "My days are like the evening shadow; I wither away like grass" (Psalm 102:11). "They will pass away like a wild flower. For the sun rises with scorching heat and withers the plant; its blossom falls and its beauty is destroyed. In the same way, the rich will fade away even while they go about their business" (James 1:10-11). "Why, you do not even know what will happen tomorrow. What is your life? You are a mist that appears for a little while and then vanishes" (4:14).

Precious to God

Though my life is brief, it is immeasurably precious to God. I know that God hears every word (see Psalm 102:17), sees every act (see 33:13-14,18), knows my thoughts (see 139:1-4), and, while I number my days, numbers the hairs on my head (see Matthew 10:30). He knows my name (see John 10:3), lists my tears on His scroll (see Psalm 56:8), plans where and when I live (see Acts 17:28), oversees the moment of my death (see Psalm 139:16), sends His Son to die on the cross for me (see John 3:16), and prepares a place for me in heaven (see 14:2), even though I am but a fleeting shadow.

His fluent expression of love should set me aquiver: "The LORD your God is with you, the Mighty Warrior who saves. He will take great delight in you; in his love he will no longer rebuke you, but will rejoice over you with singing" (Zephaniah 3:17). When I picture God's rejoicing over His people with singing, I think of Snowflake Bentley. Wilson "Snowflake" Bentley, a New England farmer, couldn't get enough of snowflakes. For forty years, he ran around in the snow, raucously joyful, catching snowflakes on chilled slides and photographing them, seeking to capture for others the beauty he saw in those one-of-a-kind masterpieces of frozen crystals. Over his lifetime, he photographed more than five thousand individual snowflakes. His notes were effusive: "No. 785 is so rarely beautiful." He wrote of the "feast of [their] beauty." As I imagine Snowflake careening in the snow, giddy with joy, I marvel with the psalmist, "LORD, what are human beings that you care for them, mere mortals that you think of them? They are like a breath; their days are like a fleeting shadow" (Psalm 144:3-4). I'm like a vanishing, vaporous breath, and God cares for me.[3]

Father, my life is a fragile breath, a snowflake with speed lines,
here one moment and gone the next. But You have always
cared for withering grass and fleeting vapors. Grace me,
please, to live in the wisdom of this reality. In Jesus' name.

Brevity of Life

This week, Jesse Permann died. He was twenty-nine years old and my grandson's favorite teacher. He had been married for one year and one week. Jesse was tall, vibrant, and caring. His life made boys want to become teachers. For Jesse, life on earth is over; now he is in the presence of his Lord in heaven. His life was short but not insignificant. Death did not catch Jesse unaware.

Henry Melville wrote, "It is evident that the great thing wanted to make men provide for eternity is the practical persuasion that they have but a short time to live. They will not apply their hearts unto wisdom until they are brought to the numbering of their days."[4] God is not asking me to number my days to increase my pace but rather to examine my route, not to increase my efficiency but to see where I must make course corrections in heart, character, and actions. Recently, my husband, Roger, and I asked a young couple we have been friends with for ten years to help us evaluate our contribution and maximize the years left. We hoped their insights might unearth blind spots and help us move wisely into the future. Chris and Kathy Graff know us well; they know our hearts and vision. Even so, they asked us questions to sharpen the process. After several weeks, they met with us again. Their counsel affirmed our direction and helped us fine-tune our focus.

Father, as I number my days, may I, by Your grace, peel away
deceptions that cloud reality. I will die soon. I must grow in my
understanding of Your purposes and desires for my time on
earth. Lord, please enable me to live whatever days left to me
for Your glory.

My life on earth has a time limit, a shelf life, an expiration date. When I number my days, each day rattles with sharp significance. What does this measured span look like as I weigh the brevity of my days? When I take those last breaths, how will I—and how will God—assess the days allotted to me? Life on earth will not go on forever. Every breath is a gift. Time is flying.

CHAPTER 8

LIVING IN TIME AND ETERNITY: PHASES 1 AND 2

Sometimes I stand in the open air and slowly turn 360 degrees, taking in the enormous western Colorado sky. Often every quadrant tells a different story. Huge cumulus clouds edged in silver pile up to the south over the San Juan Mountains. I quarter-turn and see wispy clouds blown thin. To the north, brushstroke clouds run parallel to the Grand Mesa, the largest flattop mountain in the world. Our weather often comes from the west, so I look in expectation. And overhead, nearly cloudless blue mounts up, up, up.

Just as I see the rainbow and remember the Lord's covenant, I see the clouds and remember greater realities. Jesus was seen by five hundred people as He ascended into clouds like these and now sits in heaven praying for us, reigning beside the Father, our Father, and from such a cloud He will return. He will make all wrongs right. He will come from the clouds to gather His own, consummating His work. And whether He receives me from the clouds or I come to Him in death, I will be with Him forever.

I stand under this sky, these clouds, and consider the wonder of my life: I live in both time and eternity. The Scriptures make clear that eternal life doesn't begin at death but at conversion (see John 5:24). While I pad along on earth, my life is hidden in Christ, who is seated in heaven (see Colossians 3:1-3).

The word *time* forces me to face earth's brevity and limits; the word *eternity* invites me to explore the boundless geography of God. If time is like a candle burning down, eternity is like what? Who knows? Wonderful? Endlessly wonderful? Wonderful without flux or end? God, and more of God than earth can know? Both time and eternity are part of God's plan for me. This mystery is my reality. I believe that God wants me to think seriously about living simultaneously in time and eternity.

This raises questions. As I think about the rest of my life, I need to know why God has left me on earth (to live in *time*) when I have already become a citizen of heaven. How should my *eternal* life (already begun) influence my life on earth? I think of my time on earth from *conversion to death* as Phase 1. At death, I will live in my forever-home with the Lord: Phase 2. Until then, I desire to live fully on earth, in *time*, to the glory of God, with my heart and mind *set* on my forever-life in heaven. That's what the rest of this book is about.

Phase 1: Living in Time

I wonder what it would be like to stand before the Lord at the end of life and realize I missed His intention for Phase 1. What if only then did I see God-glorifying opportunities lost forever? I think on this and I'm startled: I can honor God with faith and hope, both so highly valued in God's eyes, only in Phase 1. No need for faith and hope in heaven; all I trust God for on earth will be tangible reality there. My *time* to exercise faith and hope is nearly gone. At death, the vibrant strand of faith, hope, and love is unwound. Only love will accompany me to heaven.

Whatever *time* I have left is a gift, a bequest, a responsibility, a stewardship. Time is bounded by parentheses. Time has a beginning and an end. In current culture, time is a commodity to be managed. It's said that time is money. In Jonathan Swift's *Gulliver's Travels*, the Lilliputians think Gulliver's pocket watch is his god because he consults it constantly. Time rules. The hourglass is tipped. The sand sifts, running swiftly, relentless, unstoppable. Time is limited. The end is approaching. So what view of "time" will enable me to live my earth-years well?

Timeless eternity provides insights and motivations for living wisely now.

I consider Jesus, who knew what it meant to live perfectly in both time and eternity. Jesus the Man lived on earth the way Jesus the Son lived in heaven: "Your will be done, on earth as it is in heaven" (Matthew 6:10). His food was to do the Father's will. Each day, Jesus tasted the nourishing, life-giving bread of obedience and communion. He lived with the channels open, listening, speaking, obeying, heart-eyes and heart-ears awake and responsive, coming and going at the Father's direction, never running behind. Not only was Jesus sinless, He was singular in focus. Perhaps time itself bows the knee to a man of one thing if that one thing is God.

Jesus' life in heaven informed His life on earth. Eternity shaped time. He lived in time with clarity and perspective because He knew what came next. For the joy set before Him, the perfection of heaven, the Father's smile and countless redeemed souls, He endured the Cross, scorning its shame (see Hebrews 12:2). Eternity nourished His endurance. The joy of His sure future supported Him in His agony. Reflecting on my eternal future nourishes my endurance and joy too.

Heaven looms, but I must not expect heaven on earth.

Phase 1 begins with my new birth in Christ. New life has begun; I am forgiven, redeemed. The Holy Spirit lives in me. I gain access into the

Father's presence as a favored child. The blessings list goes on and on. But as amazing as Phase 1 is, it is inherently imperfect. Though generously swept with tastes of the coming glory, Phase 1 is as fleeting as a breath and full of troubles. Expecting heaven on earth is, I suspect, the root of much unhappiness and discontent.

Nevertheless, as my friend Monica Sharman remarked, "I love thinking about Phase 1 because it implies Phase 2." For those in Phase 1, the implication is clear: Looming in splendor is Phase 2, eternal pleasures in God's holy presence.

A Breakdown of the Phases

Phase 1 began for me when, aware of and devastated by my sin, I prayed, "Lord, I want what Jesus did on the cross to count for me." Yearning for deliverance from myself, my Phase 1 life began that day in Ocean City, New Jersey. My new life in Christ is a book written page by page in personal experience, in insight, in failure, in touching others. Day after day, one page turns after another until the last page, and the book will be closed and another book opened.

Phase 2, my glory-life, asserts a rightful influence on Phase 1. God intends that Phase 2 bless me long before I die. Only eternity's big picture answers big questions: Who am I? Why am I here? What happens when I die? What does God want from me in Phase 1?

Jesus lived well; He knew the answers.

Knowing the Cross awaited Him, Jesus washed His disciples' feet (see John 13:1-16). "Jesus knew that the Father had put all things under his power, and that he had come from God and was returning to God; so he got up from the meal . . . and wrapped a towel around his waist" (verse 3). What motivates and enables a man who sees the heavy, black clouds of a torturous death massing above Him to demonstrate love and teach lessons of humility and forgiveness? The answer: Jesus knew who He was, Whose He was, why He was on earth, and where He was going for eternity. He knew His identity, mission, and destiny. God has not left me in the dark on these big questions either. My calling and end are certain. Living in that reality gives clarity and courage to Phase 1 and security and reward in Phase 2.

The remainder of this book is divided into Phase 2 and Phase 1. Phase 2 comes first. Why? While on earth, I intend to turn slow, thoughtful circles meditating on Jesus exalted in heaven. A Phase 1 informed and fueled by regular circuits through heaven is my best defense against realizing too late that I missed God's will for my life on earth. So I run the Scriptures through the waterways of my mind and heart. Contemplating my future with the exalted and enthroned Lord on high sharpens my spiritual sensibilities, warms my affections, brightens God's light in my life, sanctifies my imagination, nourishes my weary and fainting soul, quickens my conscience, helps me to connect the practical life to the greater vision and calling, sustains my hope, and balms my injury and sorrow. The taste of heaven sweetens and strengthens my days on earth, so I seek to follow the apostle Paul's injunction: "Since, then, you have been raised with Christ, set your hearts on things above, where Christ is, seated at the right hand of God. Set your minds on things above, not on earthly things. For you died, and your life is now hidden with Christ in God" (Colossians 3:1-3).

It's never too soon to contemplate, revel in, and be shaped by glory. Too soon the time to glorify God with faith, hope, and obedience is passed. Too soon it's too late to bless a fallen world.

The chapters in the Phase 1 section of the book grew organically from the questions I asked in the Garden of the Gods: "What kind of old woman will I become? Lord, how do You want me to think about the rest of my life?" The contents grew from my prayer:

> Lord, what warnings, instructions, reminders, and inspirations
> will help me walk with You and glorify You all my life? Father,
> I don't want to skitter along on the surface of life as if there

were nothing but life on earth. Help me grasp the purpose of Phase 1 that I might bring You glory in it. Shine heaven's truth, wisdom, and power on my days here. Please light the days appointed to me on earth with this great hope. Grace me to do Your will on earth with my eyes in the clouds.

PHASE 2
HEAVEN PHASE

CHAPTER 9

THE GOSPEL FROM THE OTHER SIDE

Felix flies the crop duster airplane low, very low, over our house before dropping down to spray the nearby field. A neighbor took a photo that looks as if the small yellow airplane is landing on our roof. Sometimes I wave from the yard and the yellow plane waggles. With many years of experience, Felix avoids (barely) treetops, utility wires, and our roof. I look up and see the underbelly of a yellow plane soaring in an azure sky. Felix looks down and sees spread out before him all the known world from horizon to horizon.

Perspective has to do with where I'm standing, the angle of my line of vision. So far I know the gospel only from earth. I first heard the gospel here, and I've lived the gospel here. I know the pure gospel in part. Part of what I know is tinged with this world's thinking. Though I desire to know Christ and His gospel purely, I know that from earth, I see "through a glass darkly." I take heart: Soon I will know the gospel from heaven's perspective.

I consider this: Jesus Christ's work of redemption is the center-piece of all history on earth and in heaven. As amazing as God's work of creation is, it pales in comparison to His work of redemption.

The psalmists extol the wonders of God's creative energy and His sovereign control over all things. God pushes up the mountains; He sets the boundaries of the oceans; He sends the rain and snow; He ordains the seasons; He flings the stars into space, naming each one. But when we are in heaven, an even more extraordinary place than God's glorious first creation, the focus of attention will not be on the *place* God made but on His *grace* in saving a fallen and condemned people for His glory (see Ephesians 2:7-9). Even now, here on earth, the created world waits in rapt anticipation for the complete redemption and glorification of God's people: "The creation waits in eager expectation for the children of God to be revealed" (Romans 8:19). "We know that the whole creation has been groaning as in the pains of childbirth right up to the present time. Not only so, but we ourselves, who have the firstfruits of the Spirit, groan inwardly as we wait eagerly for our adoption to sonship, the redemption of our bodies" (verses 22-23).

In Phase 2, the redeemed, a people rescued from sin's dominion, marked and set apart by the Holy Spirit, forgiven and saved by the mercy and grace of God alone, stand before the Lord God and host of heaven. There every face will reflect the beauty of the Lord Jesus, glory upon glory, His love beyond measure displayed in a people, once renegade, now transformed into the likeness of Christ, their Savior (see 1 John 3:2). And I'm not the only one who stands in stunned amazement.

Angels, all creation, and the "rulers and authorities in the heavenly realms" gape. Paul wrote,

> Although I am less than the least of all the Lord's people, this grace was given me: to preach to the Gentiles the boundless riches of Christ, and to make plain to everyone the administration of this mystery, which for ages past was kept hidden in God, who created all things. His intent was that now, through the church, the manifold wisdom of God should be made known to the rulers and authorities in the

heavenly realms, according to his eternal purpose that he accomplished in Christ Jesus our Lord. (Ephesians 3:8-11)

John Henry Jowett refers to Dr. R. W. Dale's beautiful exposition of this passage:

> Dr. Dale speaks about the redeemed pilgrims of time telling inhabitants of the heavenly city, who have never known our estate, who have never known our sin, the story of redemption, and of how our hunger was met and how our peace was renewed; and they will tell the pilgrims about the unclouded day, about the faraway time when sin had not fallen upon the world, and all about the wonderful developments and experiences of the unsullied life.[1]

Dr. Dale paints a beautiful picture from Ephesians 3:7-12 of believers in heaven telling our stories of redemption to the inhabitants of heaven. Was there ever a story like the Cross? Were there ever stories like ours of grace upon grace? Those heavenly beings—who never lived on earth, who never sinned, who never knew or needed grace—now hear our stories and praise God with each new accounting. I imagine the rulers and authorities in the heavenly realms leaning forward to ask, "Tell us how He saved you. Tell us how He met with you when you sinned. How did He help you when you were afraid? Tell us everything about His grace that was always there."

O, the manifold wisdom of God.

In Phase 2, I enter my place of endless delight: wonders unveiled, springs unstopped, truths perceived, unbounded communion enjoyed with the Lord and others. There I will understand and glory in my story. My life on earth will come into focus without distortion. The pain of life, so seemingly senseless, will emerge in sparkling clarity with meaning. I will see that nothing came to me from caprice or malice; all came from the hand of a good and wise God. The tapestry woven out of sight is now revealed. Threads I thought so harsh and coarse are transformed into silken warp and woof. Colors, so discordant, now harmonize.

I think heaven will be full of earth — the best parts, parts closest to heaven. I ponder Malachi 3:16 in this regard: "Those who feared the LORD talked with each other, and the LORD listened and heard. A scroll of remembrance was written in his presence concerning those who feared the LORD and honored his name." When believers gather and talk about the things of God, He takes special notice and delight. The scribes of heaven record those sweet conversations. I suspect there are scrolls in heaven inscribed with some of *my* conversations with friends. A scenario forms in my mind: In heaven, a scroll will be drawn from an urn and read, "September 8, 2011, at Panera Bread: Monica Sharman and Jean Fleming talked about being a *fragrance* to God as well as a *fragrance* to people. Monica said . . ."

Bits and pieces, shreds of conversation and shards of insights, will be handled in heaven's golden light. The redeemed, as well as the rulers and authorities of heaven, will tell the gospel story from their unique perspective. And we will all hoot and cheer and praise God forever and ever.

I've placed these two brief Phase 2 chapters before Phase 1 as a reminder and a check on my perspective — a reminder that the most Spirit-sensitive believer on earth — who studies and ponders, who lives most fully in the gospel — has merely nibbled the firstfruits of the heavenly feast. As I return to these Phase 2 chapters, I acknowledge that I see only the underbelly of gospel-glories. Only in heaven will I see clearly and fully, but I intend to turn my earth-gaze toward heaven more and more. Heaven's perspective is meant to touch earth, to rain down, to rout nonchalance and keep me moving. I return to Phase 2 often because Phase 1 matters.

The inexhaustible and ever more dazzling story of heaven — the gospel, told and retold — will be eternal meat and drink. What a plotline: The King of heaven comes as sacrificial Lamb. God lives among His created ones. He redeems enemies, adopts them as His dear children, and gives them a forever-home with Himself. Every telling and every hearing of this story will set off cataracts of praise to God Most High, our Savior and Redeemer, our exalted King. Eternal bliss and wonder. This story is richer with every encounter.

Father, please give me a more heavenly perspective. I know that in heaven I will understand and appreciate Your grace and unfailing love in ways I can't muster on earth. I feel my denseness and the smog of earth severely. I yearn for that day when the scales are removed, the film that clouds my eyes is washed away, and Your light floods in to lighten my soul. Until then, open the eyes of my heart, Lord. Someday soon I will join the inhabitants of heaven in praising You with the depth of understanding, appreciation, wonder, and zeal that You deserve. Until then, thank You for the Cross. Thank You for the Resurrection. Thank You for good news of forgiveness. Thank You for the Holy Spirit indwelling. Thank You for the Word. Thank You for the church, the body of Christ. Thank You for giving me a future and a hope. Thank You.

CHAPTER 10

GLORY DAYS: ENTER HIS PRESENCE

From my breakfast nook window, I see the holy whiteness of the San Juan Mountains. It is the end of April, and fresh snow lights the peaks. My eyes travel the ground, past the lichen-rich rock wall my husband built, past the iris weeks away from blooming, past the neighbor's lawn, past the bare plowed field to the trees and houses at the end of our street, before resting on the sharp angles of blinding white. The mountains on the horizon are the finale of my gaze. Though the mountains seem close today, many fields and houses separate me from their base, a forty-minute drive away. I consider the many layers between me and the gleaming whiteness and think about the layers of days in Phase 1 until I enter the Lord's presence. And I entertain the glorious reality: Because I am in Christ, soon I will see Him in heaven.

I wonder how I will first see Jesus there. Will He come as the Lamb slain with pierced hands outstretched? Will He come as the Elder Brother ushering me into the Father's presence, or as the Bridegroom welcoming His beloved? Or will I enter His presence, a subject before her King? Will I rush into His arms, or will I fall on my face before Him?

When Isaiah the prophet (see Isaiah 6:1-8) and the apostle John (see Revelation 1:9-18) saw Jesus in His glory, they were overcome. John saw Jesus in His blinding holiness and fell at His feet as though dead. The glory, the soul-rocketing holiness and beauty of God, the sheer intensity of unadulterated, unalloyed life, sucked John's breath from him and left him limp:

> I saw . . . someone like a son of man, dressed in a robe reaching down to his feet and with a golden sash around his chest. The hair on his head was white like wool, as white as snow, and his eyes were like blazing fire. His feet were like bronze glowing in a furnace, and his voice was like the sound of rushing waters. In his right hand he held seven stars, and coming out of his mouth was a sharp, double-edged sword. His face was like the sun shining in all its brilliance. (Revelation 1:12-16)

What happened next connects me to the Jesus I know; this amazing, glowing, blazing, booming, shining Being placed His hand on the prostrated John and said, "Do not be afraid. I am the First and the Last. I am the Living One; I was dead, and now look, I am alive for ever and ever! And I hold the keys of death and Hades" (Revelation 1:17-18). Jesus, as I know Him, ever reaching down, coming down, stooping down to wash feet or write with His finger in the dirt, or to touch one flattened by life—or by glory. Even from the throne, Jesus tenderly ministers to His own.

What will it be like to enter His presence in heaven? I don't know. What I do know is that I don't deserve to be there.

I Stand Before Him Forgiven

He is holy, and heaven is His holy home. Now it is my home too. I stand in His presence, a sinner saved by grace. While on earth, passages about His forgiveness sometimes moved me to grateful sobs, but the gratitude and wonder I felt on earth will pale compared with what I will feel in heaven. Welcomed as His child, fully accepted on Christ's merit alone, I sink to my knees, grateful for Christ's blood that washed me clean. He sees no sin in me. I am robed with the righteousness of Christ. There is no reproach or condemnation. The choking waves of gratitude I felt (too infrequently) on earth will be purely and intensely felt and expressed in heaven.

> Blessed is the one whose transgressions are forgiven, whose sins are covered. Blessed is the one whose sin the LORD does not count against him and in whose spirit is no deceit. (Psalm 32:1-2)

> In him we have redemption through his blood, the forgiveness of sins, in accordance with the riches of God's grace that he lavished on us. With all wisdom and understanding. (Ephesians 1:7-8)

And Jesus comes and wipes my tears. The imagery is tender: "The Lamb at the center of the throne will be their shepherd; 'he will lead them to springs of living water. And God will wipe away every tear from their eyes'" (Revelation 7:17). Thank You, Jesus. Thank You.

Why are there tears in heaven? Perhaps tears of joy and relief, tears of gratitude, or remnant tears from earthly suffering or grief. Or, when I am fully present to Him and Him to me, will I weep that I lived so weakly for Him on earth? Will I regret my apathy, inattentiveness, and sloth? Will memories surface—times I shrunk back from speaking or lived without regard to promised resources? Will crying last or be quickly banished? All I know is that by the time God brings me to the Holy City, the New Jerusalem, "'He will wipe every tear from their eyes. There will be no more death' or mourning or crying or pain, for the old order of things has passed away" (Revelation 21:4). Earth's grief in every form will vanish.

My sin behind me, I stand before Him robed in righteousness. I am like Him (see 1 John 3:2). I am the grateful recipient of the unthinkable swap. He took my sin upon Himself and gave me His righteousness (see 2 Corinthians 5:21). I am welcomed into heaven not because I am good or because my good outweighs my bad but because *He is good*, thoroughly and completely. And here in the presence of the Lamb of God, I understand the cost of the exchange as I never could on earth. Grace! "And so we will be with the Lord forever" (1 Thessalonians 4:17).

With Him to See His Glory

What do I make of Jesus' prayer "Father, I want those you have given me to be with me where I am, and to see my glory, the glory you have given me because you loved me before the creation of the world" (John 17:24)? This is my eternal destiny, my eternal privilege, and my eternal joy. Jesus wants me to be with Him and see His glory. The eternal Son of God, the fullness and embodiment of all grace and truth, wants me to be with Him forever. The One of whom it is written, "The Son is the radiance of God's glory and the exact representation of his being, sustaining all things by his powerful word. After he had provided purification for sins, he sat down at the right hand of the Majesty in heaven" (Hebrews 1:3), wants me to be there, with Him, to see His glory forever.

> Lord Jesus, until that day when I enter Your presence and see Your glory, please show me more of Your glory here on earth. Pull back curtains, throw open doors, shine Your light in my direction. As I contemplate enjoying You forever, cause that oil of gladness (see Hebrews 1:9; Isaiah 61:3; Psalm 23:5) to overflow into Phase 1, my dust-life. Glory-days are coming. Shine on me today.

Enjoying God Forever

The veil is lifted; the haze is gone. I see with clarity. All that was promised is now vibrant reality. I see the Lord, the One I loved without seeing (see 1 Peter 1:8), now fully and visibly present. He is more glorious than my earthbound mind could conceive. Now is my time for enjoying Him forever.

Enjoy. What a word! All the words associated with *enjoy* (pleasure, delight, rejoice, make happy) are gold-tinged and resound like choirs and stars singing together. Redeemed, unable to suppress face-engulfing smiles and from-the-toes laughter, I will pinch myself because too good to be true is better than I ever imagined. And I will enjoy the Lord forever, bubbling joy, cataracts pouring forth. This is what I was made for.

Sometimes when I hear astronomers speak with awe-filled wonder of the beauty they see through their high-powered telescopes or mathematicians extol the elegance of some equation, I think of the eternity before me to observe and celebrate the beauty of the Lord. Only God Himself is great enough to occupy our eternal attention without disappointment. In company with others, I will revel in the glories of His unfathomable love and loveliness, wisdom, and power. There no voice will have even a hint of lethargy; no tainted motivations remain to mar words and actions. Once in heaven, I will live in the richness I caught glimpses of and merely nibbled as firstfruits on earth. Soon the layers of "miles" between me and the holy mountains will dissolve. Soon I will live in God's holy presence, my tears wiped dry, my earthly service done. Captivated by His glory, I will enjoy Him forever.

PHASE 1
A BEAUTIFUL LIFE
IN A FALLEN WORLD

CHAPTER 11

BEAUTIFULL—LIVING IN THE FULLNESS OF WHAT CHRIST WON FOR ME

Praise be to the God and Father of our Lord Jesus Christ,
who has blessed us in the heavenly realms with every
spiritual blessing in Christ.

EPHESIANS 1:3

As a teenager, I once walked on a golf course with a small New Testament, dipping in here and there. Unfortunately, I read it to an unwired heart. I found it dry and dull and incomprehensible. I experienced the same disconnect every morning in school when we took turns reading a psalm after the Pledge of Allegiance. I, like most of my classmates, didn't relish standing up front to read and usually chose—and raced through—the shortest psalm. Only after God adopted me into His family did He connect the circuits and plug in the electricity. The Holy Spirit flooded in, flipping switches in mind and spirit, waking me out of a dead sleep.

When He moves into a life, He comes with a truckload of blessings. I am blessed with every spiritual blessing in Christ. But I will not live a beautiful life in a fallen world unless I live in the FULLness Jesus won for me at the cross: "In Christ all the fullness of the Deity lives in bodily form, and in Christ you have been brought to fullness. He is the head over every power and authority" (Colossians 2:9-10). The Amplified Version says it this way: "You are in Him, made full *and* having come to fullness of life [in Christ you too are filled with the Godhead—Father, Son and Holy Spirit—and reach full spiritual stature]" (verse 10). Filled. Full.

> O Lord, why, then, do I often live as a pauper? How can I live more fully in the expensively purchased family treasures? Fill me with all fullness.

Mindful: Identity in Christ

My friend Nancy Lamar wisely said that doors of nursing homes should be decorated to remind those who pass that the infirm were not always so vague, nearly nameless:

This woman raised eight children and got her GED at sixty-two years of age.

This man fought in Sicily and North Africa, carried a wounded eighteen-year-old farm boy to safety, and got a Purple Heart.

This man was married to the same woman for seventy years, is a recent widower, and put six kids through college (only three were his own).

Do all old people blur together in the minds of those who pass them? Of course identity isn't just an issue associated with age. It isn't just that others don't know who we are; we wonder about it ourselves. From our earliest days *we* need to know who we are. The trouble is that no one can tell us. Not really. I am more than my parents' child, my husband's wife, my children's mother. My accomplishments don't define me; neither do my failures. I am more than my body and more than my intellect, my body type, my contribution. I am more than I know.

> Lord God, tell me who I am. Then, once You've told me, please give me grace to take it in and live in that reality. Even after all these years, the comments and attitudes of others still form part of my sense of who I am. You say that I am precious in Your sight (see Isaiah 43:4), that my old life is gone and that a new life has begun (see 2 Corinthians. 5:17), that You chose me to belong to You before You created the world (see Ephesians 1:4). You love me and care for me as an individual, but You have also placed me into a family, a body, a kingdom. I am never alone because You will never leave me. I am not an island because I am part of a living organism, the church. Even if no one else is physically near, I am as vitally connected as arm to shoulder, thumb to hand, to all believers throughout all of time — past, present, and future. I am blessed in Christ to have both an individual identity and a corporate identity. Hallelujah!

My circumstance will change, but not my identity. I belong to Christ forever; I am His redeemed and adopted child even if I am unknown by all around me. Even if no one knows the story of my life, the Lord will not forget me. Even if I forget my own name, He will claim me. I am His.

Phase 1 is the time to live ever more fully my identity in Christ. Now is the time to refuse outside voices and the persistent inner voice, time to keen in on *His* voice, to live ever more fully in the quiet joy and peace of belonging to Him.

In the Fullness of His Forgiveness

An accident, a front tooth broken off at the gum line. My treatment plan was involved and lengthy. While I sat in the chair, the only gray head in sight, waiting to have my braces cranked another notch, the Christian song "What Sin?" played over the sound system. The lyrics touched me and I began to cry. The message of the song is that when we stand before the Lord knowing well our sinfulness and knowing well that we deserve condemnation, the Lord says, "What sin?"

What sin?

Not for the first time, the realization of the complete forgiveness in Christ brought me to great heaving sobs. The orthodontist, passing by the chair, came over in concern: "Did we make your braces too tight?"

"He chose us in him before the creation of the world to be holy and blameless in his sight" (Ephesians 1:4). "If you, LORD, kept a record of sins, Lord, who could stand? But with you there is forgiveness, so that we can, with reverence, serve you" (Psalm 130:3-4).

> Father God, Lord Jesus, indwelling Spirit, thank You for full forgiveness. Thank You for the sacrifice of Christ, the cleansing power of His blood, the righteousness of Christ that now clothes me. Please help me live more and more fully free, clean and joyful in this reality.

In the Fullness of His Spirit

I remind myself that Jesus is closer to me than He was to the Twelve before the Holy Spirit came upon them. They saw Him with their eyes and heard Him with their ears, but I know Him Spirit to spirit. The Spirit indwells me and I have the mind of Christ within. Christ within expresses Himself to me and through me to my world. I want to cooperate with God's intention that Christ live His life through me all the way to the grave. In that way, I will be a fragrance (see 2 Corinthians 2:14-16), a letter (see 3:1-3), a reflection (see verse 18), a jar of clay holding a treasure (see 4:7). "Christ *in* you, the hope of glory" (Colossians 1:27, emphasis added).

> Father, I am a jar of clay with a treasure inside. I want to live wide open to the Spirit's influence in my life when I sense His presence and ministry in me and through me, in plodding times when executing glamorless daily responsibilities, and in those deep-water times when life is crashing in and the bottom is falling out. Grace me, Lord. Unexpectedly, sometimes the hardest times to consent to the Spirit's vibrant life within are days marked by no special grief or joy, days like most days, "every day" days. Fill me.

Maturity in Christ and being full of the Spirit are not synonymous. The newest believer can live in the fullness of the Spirit and often does. But to live in the fullness of the Spirit day after day is the work of a lifetime. Listening. Responding. Repenting. Surrendering. Listening. Learning. Changing my mind. Changing my plans, my actions. Listening . . .

In the Fullness of His Word

Living in the fullness of the Spirit and the fullness of the Word of God are much the same, requiring the same receptivity and response. When I read the Holy Scriptures, I read the "coming down from heaven" words from the undisturbed, incorruptible center of all existence. God calls me to live fully in these riches (see Colossians 3:16).

Jesus told Nicodemus, "Very truly I tell you, we speak of what we know, and we testify to what we have seen, but still you people do not accept our testimony. I have spoken to you of earthly things and you do not believe; how then will you believe if I speak of heavenly things?

No one has ever gone into heaven except the one who came from heaven — the Son of Man" (John 3:11-13).

The "we" is Jesus and the Spirit, both sent by the Father to tell us the truth. Their testimony is meant to blow away the disillusioning fog that descended upon us in our corrupted state, that deceptive haze in which we stumble along, distracted and oblivious. Jesus and the Spirit leave the glories of heaven to deliver a message: the Word of God, the truth of God. Unfortunately, too often this Word is greeted with skepticism, antagonism, or a wan and watery acceptance. The Word of God rarely finds the rapturous reception that Word from heaven deserves.

> Words from heaven, dwell in me richly. Lord, I want to do more than read Your words. I want to draw them up like a sponge, draw them up like jasmine honey through a straw, marinate in them, imprint them on my bones, spirit, and mind. Please, Lord, throw the switch. Charge my circuits with Your Holy Word. Please fill me.

CHAPTER 12

THE MINISTRY OF COUNTENANCE AND SPIRIT: GLORIFYING GOD AND BLESSING OTHERS

God, who said, "Let light shine out of darkness," made his light shine in our hearts to give us the light of the knowledge of God's glory displayed in the face of Christ.

2 CORINTHIANS 4:6

A person's wisdom brightens their face and changes its hard appearance.

ECCLESIASTES 8:1

I believe there is a ministry of countenance. I came to this conclusion while speaking at a conference where I knew no one. When I got up to speak, I was tempted to bolt. The faces of the women looking up at me were grim. They had invited me to travel to their city to speak to them, but I wondered if they'd regretted it even before I began. Bravely, I launched into my presentation. And there, over to the left a few rows back, I spotted her. She was alert, attentive, leaning forward, giving every impression that she was hopeful that I might say something worthwhile. She nodded from time to time. She took notes. She even smiled several times. Bless her. Her countenance ministered to me as I came to minister to those women.

> Lord, I want my face to minister to people, whether to someone delivering a talk or to the person sitting across from me. I know that the human face is a transmitter and a receiver, always sending and picking up messages. Will my expression encourage the speaker to continue and elaborate, or will it shut them down? Will my face serve the purposes of God? Will it communicate that the God of love lives in me? Lord, I'm too often so thoughtless in face-to-face encounters. In the years remaining, please express Your love and concern for people through me. I offer my face to You. Make it a channel of blessing.

Once when I was sharing a concern, our daughter-in-law Yasuko so totally connected that I felt as if my pain was running through currents to her. Without saying a word, she shared my hurt. Her countenance became a great and palpable kindness. As I looked across the table at Yasuko, her face became the face of Christ to me. I saw in her expression the listening and loving of the Lord Jesus Himself. This is what the Lord does: He enters in; He engages.

I've wondered what the woman taken in adultery saw in the face of Jesus (see John 8:3-11). What did the leper see (see Luke 5:12-14)? When the woman at the well conversed with Jesus, did His expression prepare a space in her heart for the penetrating words He spoke (see John 4:1-26)? Was His countenance an offering of hospitality, a welcoming connection? There is great possibility in face-to-face encounter.

The psalmist prayed, "Let the light of your face shine on us" (Psalm 4:6). In Psalm 80, the request is repeated three times: "Restore us, O God; make *your face shine on us*, that we may be saved" (see verses 3,7,19, emphasis added).

A similar plea is expressed in the priestly blessing:

The LORD bless you, and keep you;
The LORD *make His face shine on you*, and be gracious to you;
The LORD *lift up His countenance on you*, and give you peace.
(Numbers 6:24-26, NASB, emphasis added)

What exactly were the psalmist and the priest asking for? The Amplified Version expresses it this way:

The Lord make His face to shine upon *and* enlighten you and be gracious (kind, merciful, and giving favor) to you;

The *Lord lift up His [approving] countenance upon* you and give you peace (tranquility of heart *and* life continually). (Numbers 6:25-26, emphasis added)

Like me, they yearned for God's approving look, His warm acceptance and fellowship. The imagery of the smiling countenance contains so many blessings: favor, restoration, salvation, victory, and deliverance. How great is my need for the restoring favor of the Lord's smile.

When I ask for the light of God's countenance, I know that it comes to me by grace. God's approving look, His smile, is undeserved. God is not impressed with me. Though I can't earn His smile, I can't live a beautiful life apart from it. A beautiful life blossoms out of experiencing the benefits of His "glorious grace, which he has freely given us in the One he loves" (Ephesians 1:6). It gives me a great sense of security to know that God's smile comes to me because I am in Christ, not because I'm adorable. It is so hard to be adorable all the time.

"It was not by their sword that they won the land, nor did their arm bring them victory; it was your right hand, your arm, and the *light of your face*, for you loved them" (Psalm 44:3, emphasis added). As I bask in the light of God's countenance, something happens in me. I am changed as I linger. I look at the Lord, and His beauty shines on me and in me. The apostle Paul expressed it this way: "All of us who have had that veil removed can see and reflect the glory of the Lord. And the Lord—who is the Spirit—makes us more and more like him as we are changed into his glorious image" (2 Corinthians 3:18, NLT).

Those of us who know God, who have been saved from destruction and eternal lostness, who carry around in our bodies the treasure of knowing the gospel and the Holy Spirit Himself, should radiate something of that wonder. Paul wrote that we "have this treasure in jars of clay" (4:7). How could there not be a certain "glory" about us? Surely some radiance should be seeping out between our ears.

Although I've heard variations on "If you're saved and you know it, tell your face," I'm often unaware that I've let my face go slack. But when I remember that my countenance can minister to others the love, compassion, and interest of God, I can tune in and turn my stony face into an organ of blessing.

I remember a few times when one of my kids came to me to ask, "Are you mad, Mom?"

"No. Why do you ask?"

"Well . . . your face."

As social creatures, humans read one another unconsciously. My body language and expression telegraph signals to those around me. What message am I sending?

When I think of the ministry of countenance, two faces come to mind. One, Karl Kratts, a small man in his late nineties who glowed. My husband loved to see him coming toward us at church, spry and beaming, with one finger in the air: "I'm going to see Him soon." At a hundred one years old, Karl left this earth to be with his Savior. Karl's daughter commented that when he spoke of his conversion, it always sounded as if it had just happened. Karl never lost his redemption-wonder, and it showed in his face.

Another luminous countenance from a former church is Mary Jane Ponten, a widow who was born with cerebral palsy. Her face is screwed up in a perpetual smile. She is witty and spritely. In spite of considerable health challenges, Mary Jane travels internationally doing mission work among the handicapped. What touches me most profoundly is her joyful face. Neither Karl nor Mary Jane will make the cover of *People* magazine, but to me their faces are truly beautiful countenances that minister the joy of the Lord.

My husband and I often reflect on the rarity of seeing a radiant older person, and I remind myself that the challenges of age don't release me from responsibility to live for the benefit of others, the glory of God, and the advancement of His kingdom. The generations following me are watching and listening. Will my countenance communicate confidence in God's goodness, satisfaction with His presence, promise, and provision? Will His light shine in me?

May the coming generations always have a Karl Kratts or Mary Jane Ponten to remind them there is a gracious God in heaven. May I be one of those people.

CHAPTER 13

DEEP TRACKS: A SCAFFOLD OF DISCIPLINE AND CREATIVITY

Our son Graham and his wife, Yasuko, live in Japan. While we were there on a recent visit, we took care of the kids while Graham and Yasuko went on a date at a mountain restaurant in Okutama. The restaurant owner, a ninety-seven-year-old man, sat with our son, pointing out a tree he planted thirty-five years ago and the carefully chosen rocks he'd brought from the mountains to landscape his grounds. I was intrigued as Graham and Yasuko recounted the content of their conversation with him, so I tried to capture something of it in a "poem":

Old man, owner of Okutama restaurant,
His life a scaffold of discipline and creativity:
Trees planted, rocks placed.
Every day an offering of various-sameness:
Exercise, one hour,

Three newspapers read,
A poem written,
Seventy omanju* made,
Two hundred on weekends.
Today on a mountain bench
He talks to a young foreigner
And shows him a tree he
Planted thirty-five years ago
And says he wrote a song to every
rock.
*omanju: a Japanese dessert

I used the phrases "a scaffold of discipline and creativity" and "every day an offering of various-sameness" to express what I find so attractive about his life. Pulitzer Prize–winning author Annie Dillard wrote,

> What then shall I do this morning? How we spend our days is, of course, how we spend our lives. What we do with this hour, and that one, is what we are doing. A schedule defends from chaos and whim. It is a net for catching days. It is a scaffolding on which a worker can stand and labor with both hands at sections of time.[1]

At ninety-seven, will I be able to write a poem capturing the scaffold of my life? How would I want it to read?

Old woman, keeper of a house,
Keeper of her heart,
Lover of one man.
Her life a scaffold of discipline and creativity:
Morning after morning: Jesus.
Her heart Bible-bent.
Prayers rise.

Every day an offering of various-sameness:
One hour of exercise (Oh, I wish!),
Dishes washed, laundry hung,
Generations welcomed,
Fed.
A good book read.
Art made life,
Life made art.
Preparation made for forever.

My intent for this book is to explore content worth returning to for the rest of my life—content to inspire, clarify, realign, and fortify me to live Christ and His purposes to the end. So I ask myself, *Why would I come back to this chapter throughout my life?*

Life Well Lived Wears Deep Tracks

A deep track can be nothing more than a rut, unproductive and perhaps even destructive. I ponder, *Well-worn tracks in what direction?*

- The path to the prayer closet pounded hard, indented
- The circuit from the Bible to the heart a sanctified-channel
- A trail of faith-and-love choices to the glory of God

This doesn't happen without creativity and discipline. Creativity and discipline are invigorating and stabilizing counterpoints to one another. Without discipline and creativity, can anyone live a beautiful life in a fallen world?

The world quite literally fell in on one man in Haiti. A survivor of the 2010 earthquake, head of a music school, Juilliard-trained and blind, was trapped in rubble for eighteen hours. During that time, he constructed a "scaffold of various-sameness." He structured his hours: He prayed and meditated for twenty minutes; then he played, note by note, various classical pieces in his mind for forty minutes. He passed his earthquake-prison time repeating this pattern, a configuration of discipline and creativity.

The creativity I applaud here is not that he is a musician or that he played music in his mind but rather that he creatively determined how he would use his time when few options were open to him. I imagine the terror of being confined to a small space, not knowing if rescuers would come. The physical dilemma is undeniable, but the greater challenge is managing the mind and spirit. Panic and despair are threats as dangerous as the weight of debris and the need for food and water. Although I might never suffer through disaster like this courageous man did, everyday life provides ample challenges and opportunities to choose the shape my life will take.

Various-Sameness

Various-sameness is a characteristic of the created world. The sun rises every morning, though at a different point on the horizon. Its rise is predictable. I may glory in the radiant dawning if I take pause to observe it, but I'm never surprised to see it. I glory in the various-sameness of a strand of Black-Eyed Susans in my yard, each flower different in particulars, all the same in general. I love the various-sameness of living my adult life with one man, the same man, a man who is ever-changing, growing.

What will be the same, day after day, in all life's rich variation? The challenge is to choose the scaffolding wisely. When I look back over my life, what will be the shape that emerges?

There are two kinds of scaffolding. One is a static schedule, daily or weekly tasks performed at set times. Sometimes the culture supports this scaffold, but even the British ritual of four o'clock tea is endangered. When I was a girl, an unwritten framework shaped a woman's week. I remember hanging out clothes for my mother, gazing down the backyards in my neighborhood and seeing white sheets flapping from every line. Monday was wash day. Tuesday was ironing. I'm unaware of obvious patterns today, so I must create my own. My friend's parents devised a weekly menu and shopping list to simplify life as they aged. When Jeanne's mother died, her father continued an established pattern. Firm structures serve young families as well.

The second kind of scaffolding is a clear structure of mission and values. Because I'm engaged with young moms, I meet with them at their convenience: during children's naptimes or when childcare is available. My scaffold, a firm structure, purposeful with arbitrary time slots, reminds me what's valuable and necessary. The apostle Paul calls me to "careful" living—to thoughtful, deliberate, earnest, even creative living. He wrote, "Be very careful, then, how you live—not as unwise but as wise, making the most of every opportunity, because the days are evil. Therefore do not be foolish, but understand what the Lord's will is" (Ephesians 5:15-17).

A Disciplined Life

Spiritual disciplines are life habits, which ground and deepen me in the faith and help me resist random currents. Disciplines are habits with a purpose. My decision to meet with the Lord every morning rises out of freedom and desire. It is my aspiration to draw near to Him, to shut out distractions the best I can, to listen, to speak. To say yes to this date with God means I say no to whatever competes with it. Every discipline is a yes and a no. The trick is to match the right response to the right commitment or diversion.

Creativity is an essential part of spiritual discipline and the spiritual disciplines. It is a tribute to human creativity that we can always find a way to do what we really want to do, to do what we really think is important. This is about discerning the path that takes me where I want to go and then tramping that path again and again.

Daniel prayed three times a day from his upstairs room (see Daniel 6:10). I suspect it required both creativity and discipline for

Daniel to establish and maintain this schedule. New patterns are hard to establish. I tried for a while to intercede for family when I turned on the lights at dawn and twilight, inspired by Exodus 30:7-8: "Aaron must burn fragrant incense on the altar every morning when he tends the lamps. He must burn incense again when he lights the lamps at twilight so incense will burn regularly before the LORD for the generations to come." But even established disciplines regularly need an enlivening charge. Just as creativity without discipline cannot be sustained, discipline without creativity can become tedious and dreary.

Creative and Disciplined

It is one thing to be creative in the artistic sense, a craftsman with paintbrush or violin or hammer; it is something else to make your *life* art, a thing of beauty. Although Jesus was a craftsman, a carpenter, His greatest artistic achievement was a life well lived. His everyday personal interactions were examples of a creative mind and soul. His speech was vivid, laced with unforgettable images that penetrated the mind like well-driven nails. To one person, He spoke of being "born again" (John 3:3), to another of "living water" (4:10), and to another of "whitewashed tombs" (Matthew 23:27). Jesus used images tailored to the hearer for maximum impact. He was also a disciplined man, a man of the Word, of prayer and fasting, of public and private worship. His life, as recorded in the Gospels, is a scaffold of discipline and creativity, a work of art.

> Father, when life accelerates, be my perimeter protection as
> I strive to erect and maintain a scaffold for Your purposes and
> glory. When life falls in around me, when rubble pins and
> I breathe dust in darkness, suffuse my days with Your creative
> light and possibility. Please help me live well a string of days
> until I come to You. In Jesus' name.

CHAPTER 14

BLESSED IMAGINATION: LIVING A REVERENT AND KIND LIFE

*What is imagination but a reflection of our yearning to
belong to eternity as well as to time?*

STANLEY KUNITZ

John Ruskin said that an unimaginative person can never be reverent
or kind.[1] I believe that he is right. An unimaginative person is confined
to the dry dust of what is concrete and at hand. He or she cannot be
transported into the world of the heart or spirit.

Can anyone revere an invisible holy God apart from the ministry
of imagination?

Can anyone feed on the Scriptures apart from a consecrated stream
of vivid meditation?

Can anyone show sympathy unless they can imagine the plight of
another?

Can anyone live a beautiful life in a fallen world apart from applied imagination?

Although it seems that some believers view the imagination as subversive, I believe that God gives imagination to lead us out of color-less and constricted lives. Perhaps when others think "imagination," they think in terms of making up something that doesn't exist, some-thing fictitious. What I mean is using my imagination to lay hold and engage more fully what is real and true. "We fix our eyes not on what is seen, but on what is unseen, since what is seen is temporary, but what is unseen is eternal" (2 Corinthians 4:18). Percy Bysshe Shelley wrote in *A Defence of Poetry* that we must learn to "imagine that which we know."[2]

I seek to accept, believe, and embrace what God says even though much of the content is invisible or future. The spiritually disciplined imagination is a gift of the Holy Spirit to enable me to more fully enter into invisible and future realities.

> Father, develop in me a nimble and disciplined sanctified imagination to the end that I might escape the stifling prison of self, bring spiritual truth to vibrant life, and live in time and eternity simultaneously.

Escaping the Stifling Prison of SELF

Nothing is more natural—and sinful—than self-absorption. Without imagination, I am trapped, spinning on the axis of self-interest. Only when I can enter the world of another, putting myself in his or her concerns and feelings, can I slip the confining straitjacket of self. This is, of course, the Christlikeness that I am called to emulate: "Do noth-ing out of selfish ambition or vain conceit. Rather, in humility value others above yourselves, not looking to your own interests but each of you to the interests of the others. In your relationships with one another, have the same mindset as Christ Jesus" (Philippians 2:3-5).

As I imagine how that looks in real life, two people come to mind—two people, poles apart, who have escaped the confines of self to enter into the concerns of another. The first is the little servant girl in Naaman's household (see 2 Kings 5). I know a few things about her; I must imagine the rest. The Bible says that she is a young Jewish girl taken captive and placed in Naaman's house as a servant to his wife. My imagination kicks in and I infer some details. She is a girl stripped from her own home. No parents embrace her at the end of the day or give her counsel. She has lost more than her family; she has lost the bracing security of her culture, language, and religion. Certainly, she has known fear, loneliness, confusion, and frustration. The Scriptures don't detail her duties, but I imagine her brushing her mistress's hair, gathering up the towels after her mistress bathes, and helping her into her clothes. Sometimes she just stands as unobtrusively as possible, attentive, alert to the next opportunity to serve. The little girl notices lines of anxiety etching her mistress's face, tears welling more and more often in her eyes. The servant girl enters into Naaman's wife's grief: Naaman has leprosy.

None of the words that define her (young, Jewish, girl, servant) would give her a place of influence with Naaman and his wife. But her sweet sympathy and concern persuade Naaman to seek help from a Jewish man of God. Naaman is healed, and I imagine the little girl knows a fresh measure of healing as well.

The second person with enough imagination to enter into another's world is a centurion. He is the opposite pole to the little servant girl. She is the servant who enters the concern of her master; he is the master who enters the concern of his servant (see Matthew 8:5-13). He is a man of power and authority, a Gentile whose sympathies enable him to leap over boundaries of class and race to step into another's shoes. By imagination, the rich enters the world of the poor; the healthy enters the world of the diseased.

British pastor John Henry Jowett wrote that "imagination is the exploring faculty prospecting other worlds."[3] Both Naaman's little servant girl and the Roman centurion are great examples.

The opposite extreme from these healthy prospectors is the psycho-path who is unable to feel sympathy, so cruelty and barbarity reigns. No one lives in a tinier and lonelier world than those imprisoned in self by the absence of compassion. Jowett said, "When a hallowed imagination is at work, egotism dies, and with the death of egotism, loneliness is destroyed."[4] When the "I" seed dies and is buried (see John 12:24), something happens in that sodden darkness; the seed that "dies" produces much fruit. The lonely seed is no longer alone. The "blessed imagination" liberates the self that resides at the center of a lonely universe.

Disciplined Imagination

The Holy Spirit and the Word of God feed and shape a sanctified imagination. The Word of God gives me the content; the Holy Spirit guides the process of incarnating the content in my life, making the Word flesh. Black and white marks on the pages of my Bible rise up in four and five dimensions, no longer limited to time and space as earth-lings know it. The Lord of the text compels me to be present. This is meditation in the biblical sense.

Left to myself, my imagination is a lunatic ricocheting around the walls of my mind. The wild-eyed, slobbering imagination is destructive. An untamed imagination is the playground and rat wheel for worry, lust, bitterness, greed, and unholy fantasies. Will my imagination function as a gift from God or a soul-decaying cotton candy from the Enemy?

> Spirit of God, rein in my mind, steer it within the bounds of the Word of God. Bless my imagination, that faculty that puts flesh on bones, scents the bloom, and sloshes in the colors. Engage my mind and spirit to make what is invisible visible to my heart. O Lord, apart from imagination, how do I follow the injunction,

"Since, then, you have been raised with Christ, set your hearts on things above, where Christ is, seated at the right hand of God. Set your minds on things above, not on earthly things. For you died, and your life is now hidden with Christ in God. When Christ, who is your life, appears, then you also will appear with him in glory" (Colossians 3:1-4)? May eternal realities secure their hold and blossom in my everyday earth-life.

The great Christian classic *The Pilgrim's Progress* is a wonderful example of the Spirit-controlled imagination at work. The godly John Bunyan was in prison. Many rampaging thoughts could have consumed his life from within. Instead, the good news occupied his mind and he wrote a gripping allegorical narrative based on the gospel. Or read the sermons of C. H. Spurgeon, considered the Prince of Preachers, to see the Scriptures brought to sparkling life. Spurgeon united scholarship and "consecrated ingenuity," a term he used in a lecture to his theology students.[5] His lavish meditation and disciplined imagination served his own spiritual life as well as the spiritual lives of those who heard his preaching.

Everything about the way the Lord communicates calls out to the imagination. The Scriptures are laced with types, metaphors, and similes. Jesus' parables invite intensive handling. Spurgeon contends that Jesus' miracles are "acted sermons," a summons to slow down, look deeper, and see salvation-truth dramatized. Often the Lord's expression is spare. The Bible text, clean-lined and unembellished, leaves lavish space for me to come to the same passage again and again with profit. One day, I come to the passage about Naaman's servant girl and pray for compassion. Another day, her boldness inspires me to pray for courage to speak into a situation. I notice that she moves out of her comfort zone and God uses her for His glory. Day after day, I come to pull hand over hand on the well rope, letting down the bucket again and again. Imagination allows me to live in elevations and go down into the deeps. Imagination, like a curious bent, leads me to mine the surface truth, to dig down one more layer, and another, to sift the soil for nuggets. Here I sort and savor. Here I peer into eternity, lift out the otherworldly colors, listen for the praising hosts while leaving one foot firmly planted on earth. Until I live in heaven permanently, I offer my imagination to God and ask for grace to escape self, to be both reverent and kind in Phase 1. To God's glory. It's another way of living a beautiful life in a fallen world.

CHAPTER 15

LIKE A LITTLE CHILD

The French poet priest Michel Quoist wrote,

> God says: I like youngsters. I want people to be like them.
> I don't like old people unless they are still children.
> I want only children in my Kingdom; this has been decreed
> from the beginning of time.
> Youngsters — twisted, humped, wrinkled, white-bearded —
> all kinds of youngsters, but youngsters.
> There is no changing it; it has been decided. There is room for
> no one else[1]

Quoist's poem, of course, comes from Matthew 18:3-5. Jesus said, "Unless you change and become like little children, you will never enter the kingdom of heaven. Therefore, whoever takes the lowly position of this child is the greatest in the kingdom of heaven" (Matthew 18:3-4).

I think about what a seventy-year-old child looks like. What does a thirty-year-old child look like? How do I enter the kingdom as a little child? How do I live as a little kingdom-child all my days? What are the characteristics of little children? I read what early church fathers wrote on this topic. They refer to the innocence and sweetness of little children, and I remind myself that these men were "church fathers," not fathers of little children.

Jesus wants me to change and become like a little child. "Change and become." Repent. Turn around. Change direction. Think and operate with a different mindset. Self-assertiveness and self-protectiveness must twist, turn quite around, reverse, be *converted*. Jesus says that I must humble myself like a little child. Interesting — *not* ask God to make me humble but rather humble myself. Adults in the full glory of adulthood must be converted into humble smallness again. *Teach me, Lord, what this means.*

I must learn Jesus. He perfectly models the humble child in both His physical coming and His relational living. His humility is legible in every gospel account. The Creator, the King, the Lord of lords comes to earth in holy smallness: a babe in Bethlehem. He enters the *kingdom of man* as a child so that *I* might enter the *kingdom of God* as a child. Jesus makes Himself small enough to live among us (see Philippians 2:5-8). Jesus is always, without exception, the humble child who submits to the Father's will day after day.

Jesus goes on: "And whoever welcomes one such child in my name welcomes me" (Matthew 18:5). A great reason to be childlike: Jesus identifies Himself with the little and lowly. He Himself is childlike. I'm captivated as I study, scene by scene, His time among us. He is humble in His essential nature. I'm not. I must be converted again and again. For me, humility must grow in mind and heart with careful feeding and resolute weeding. Humility is a fruit of the Spirit's activity in my life. Humility grows in the soil of surrender, trust, and obedience.

The Making of a Child

I'm wondering if the conversion of the apostle Paul is another picture worth pondering. The pre-Paul (Saul), hell-bent on persecuting followers of Jesus, is brought to a skidding halt on the road to Damascus (see Acts 9:1-18). Under blinding light and electric voice, the charging zealot in all his angry rage sinks to the ground, aware of his grievous sin and need, profoundly humbled. The big man shrinks to childlike smallness. Gone, the powerful, swaggering persecutor; now a thirty-something child is led by the hand into Damascus.

God spins out the image further. Blind Saul receives a vision: A man named Ananias will come, lay hands on him, and restore his sight. God could restore Saul's sight without help from Ananias, but I think God was reinforcing a truth: No one enters the kingdom unless he becomes like a little child. God kept Saul in a three-day solitary darkness to slay something of his pattern of self-reliance. The self-assured zealot, blinded and resighted, becomes like a child to enter the kingdom.

The apostle Paul twisted around, turned quite around, reversed course when he relinquished all he studied and worked for to become a little child in the kingdom. Paul put his adult resumé aside (see Philippians 3:4-6) to become a little child in Jesus. He wrote, "Whatever were gains to me I now consider loss for the sake of Christ. What is more, I consider everything a loss because of the surpassing worth of knowing Christ Jesus my Lord, for whose sake I have lost all things. I consider them garbage, that I may gain Christ and be found in him, not having a righteousness of my own that comes from the law, but that which is through faith in Christ—the righteousness that comes from God on the basis of faith" (verses 7-9).

A child has no platform, no achievement. Instead, a child must depend on another for all that comes to him.

Mature Childlikeness

Father, I think of the questions that motivated work on this book: What kind of old woman will I become? How do You want me to think about the rest of life? I know now that I want

to be a child, Your child, for the rest of my life. Teach me more
of what it means to mature into childhood.

Jesus calls me to mature childlikeness—not an adult who still
exists on milk, needing another to feed her, but a meat-eating child
who lives in joyful dependence on the Father. My attention must not
focus on becoming childlike but rather on enlarging my knowledge of
and confidence in my Father's care and support. I must keep coming
to Jesus for His touch.

> People were bringing little children to Jesus for him to place his
> hands on them, but the disciples rebuked them. When Jesus saw
> this, he was indignant. He said to them, "Let the little children
> come to me, and do not hinder them, for the kingdom of God
> belongs to such as these. Truly I tell you, anyone who will not
> receive the kingdom of God like a little child will never enter it."
> And he took the children in his arms, placed his hands on them
> and blessed them. (Mark 10:13-16)

Children came to Jesus; He touched them and blessed them. I first
studied the word *touched* when I prayed for Jesus' touch on my children. *Thayer's Lexicon* spins out the word *touch* in rich pictures that
inspire meditation. The meanings translate as "to fasten to; adhere to;
to fasten fire to a thing, to kindle, set on fire."[2] I prayed that Jesus
would touch my children, fasten them to Himself, ignite their spirits
with His Spirit, and set their hearts on fire. I desired that God would
put His hands on them and bless them. Now, as an adult-child, I see
my need to come, again and again, to Jesus to be fastened to Him that
He might dissolve the hard borders of self and fasten His fire to me. So
I pray for myself as I prayed for my children, "Touch me, fasten my
soul to Yourself, kindle and ignite me, bless me."

I've been blessed to see sweet crinkled, wrinkled, childlike faces lit
with Christ's burning fire, ageless spirits kindled with the Holy Spirit's

free range in their lives, eyes with hope's blaze behind them. Actual age has little to commend it. Sadly, there are children who are no longer childlike. The children the Lord fills His kingdom with are not defined by age.

Jesus invites, "Let the little children come to me" (Matthew 19:14). Small and spiritually destitute, having nothing to commend me to God, I come as a little child.

O, Lord, work Your work in me. I need to be converted, turned, reversed, over and over again, that I might become a little child in Your kingdom. I want to be an obedient, humble daughter to You like the Son You are to the Father. Lord, I need You, but I have no idea how much I need You.

CHAPTER 16

HOSPITALITY: A WELCOMING LIFE

The Father said to his servants, "Quick! Bring the best robe and put it on him. Put a ring on his finger and sandals on his feet. Bring the fattened calf and kill it. Let's have a feast and celebrate."

LUKE 15:22-23

Our son who lives in Japan will arrive soon with his middle son. I clean and shift stuff. I buy the best rice I can find. I check out a stack of children's books from the library, put together a box of art supplies for Andy, and make lists of fun things to do. I rein in my excitement, my anticipation of having them under our roof, sharing life with them, absorbing them into our home. A "welcome" sign hangs over my heart.

It strikes me that a "welcome" sign hangs over God's heart, too. After Jesus' baptism and before He began His public ministry, John the Baptist pointed two of his disciples to Jesus: "Look, the Lamb of God!" (John 1:36). The two followed Jesus (literally). When Jesus turned and asked what they wanted, they inquired, "Where are you staying?" (verse 38). There may be some deep cultural or spiritual significance to their question, but it sounds like the kind of dumb thing I say when I'm caught off guard. But the next part was full of grace and hospitality. Jesus said, "Come, and see," and they spent that day with Him. Jesus—the Creator, Sustainer, and Inheritor of all things—welcomed them into His world, His life. Soon people of all ages would be drawn to this welcoming-magnet-God.

I notice that three gospels record Jesus' hospitality to children (see Matthew 19:13-14; Mark 10:14; Luke 18:16), one of them stating, "Then people brought little children to Jesus for him to place his hands on them and pray for them. But the disciples rebuked them. Jesus said, 'Let the little children come to me, and do not hinder them, for the kingdom of heaven belongs to such as these'" (Matthew 19:13-14).

> Come, all you who are thirsty,
>> come to the waters;
> and you who have no money,
>> come, buy and eat!
> Come, buy wine and milk
>> without money and without cost.
> Why spend money on what is not bread,
>> and your labor on what does not satisfy?
> Listen, listen to me, and eat what is good,
>> and you will delight in the richest of fare.
> Give ear and come to me;
>> listen, that you may live. (Isaiah 55:1-3)

Come to me, all you who are weary and burdened, and I will give you rest. Take my yoke upon you and learn from me, for I am gentle and humble in heart, and you will find rest for your souls. (Matthew 11:28-29)

Father, You are the God of "come." *Come* is the most
welcoming word in the English language, and You issue the
invitation so liberally: "Come. Draw near. Stay. Abide." For the
rest of my life I want to respond to the wonder of Your
hospitality.

A Torn Curtain and a "Welcome" Sign

When Jesus died on the cross, the curtain separating the Holy of
Holies from the rest of the temple was torn from top to bottom (see
Matthew 27:51; Mark 15:38). This curtain set the Most Holy Place
apart in the interior of the temple. Only the High Priest entered this
Most Holy Place, and only once a year. On the Day of Atonement, the
High Priest carried blood into this holy curtained-off space. The book
of Hebrews reveals that this drama, acted out in isolation once a year,
foreshadowed Christ's atoning work as our High Priest offering His
own blood as a propitiation for our sins.

The temple curtain was tall, the top beyond man's reach. That the
curtain was torn from top to bottom is significant. I catch my breath.
The Father sees the Son's death and rips the curtain, opening access
into His presence. The door is open; the invitation stands: "Come."
This act of hospitality makes my knees weak.

Father, You welcome me into Your presence; You open Your
home and heart to me. One day I will come to live with You,
and the scent of heaven will clothe me. Until then, I come to
You in Christ's Name, a child before her Father, awkwardly
scuffing the earth at my feet. I confess, the privilege of Your
hospitality has not captured me as it should. Please stir me to
come to You through the split curtain hung with the "welcome"
sign.

Beautiful Hospitality

This hospitable God catches me off guard: He allows me the privilege of offering *Him* hospitality. Jesus said, "Anyone who loves me will obey my teaching. My Father will love him, and we will come to them and make our home with them" (John 14:23). What makes a welcoming home for the Lord?

> Father, purify my love for You and enlarge my desire to obey You. Whatever it was that made You like being in Mary and Martha's home, please develop that in my life. Make my life a hospitable home for Your indwelling.

I'm convinced that part of living a beautiful life in a fallen world is reflecting God's hospitable nature. Hospitality is a requirement for leaders in the church (see 1 Timothy 3:2; 5:10; Titus 1:8). Those who enjoy God's hospitality must extend hospitality to others: "Share with the Lord's people who are in need. Practice hospitality" (Romans 12:13). A welcoming life is more than offering a meal and a bed. When I consider the Lord's hospitality, I think of His listening ear and His self-revelation. The words *conversation* and *communion* may be the sweetest fruit of hospitality.

> Lord, do others find me approachable? Welcoming? Grow in me an ear that listens, that "hears" more than the words spoken, and lips that nourish others in the "home of my attention." Hospitality affirms another's value. Even the stranger needs the acknowledgment that dignifies. And, Lord, You say that some have entertained angels without knowing it (see Hebrews 13:2). Too often I'm distracted. Please, Lord, express Your hospitable spirit in my life.

Offering Hospitality to Myself

When a teenager questioned why she should make her bed and tidy her room when she could merely close the door on the mess, her mother replied, "It is an act of hospitality to yourself." There is profound wisdom in this mother's answer. Our homes minister to us as well as to others. *Home* and *come* are spelled alike but for the first letter. *Come* and *home* are words meant to bless us in our earthly pilgrimage. Home calls, "Come."

Even a poor mole hole can call, "Come," and stir the soul. In *The Wind in the Willows*, Kenneth Grahame describes in homey detail every significant character's dwelling. Whether Toad's grand house or Mole's underground run, the care with which they made their homes reflects their deep emotional longing to be ensconced there and to share it with friends. In a moving scene, Mole trails his friend Rat through a snowy woods. Rat is hunched, pressing on in the storm, his one thought: to reach the pleasant warmth of home. Mole is trudging along behind, disheartened, when a scent arrests him. He tingles with electric response as instinct tells him that his home is near. Mole hears his home calling, "Come!" Rat, unaware of Mole's homesickness, cheerily propels him on, away from his beloved home. When Rat finally understands, he comforts the sobbing Mole, and they backtrack to spend the night in mole's shabby, much-loved home.

My mother was a widow for twenty-five years. Although she lived alone, she cooked full, well-balanced meals and kept a neat house. Her friends asked, "Why trouble yourself to cook when you could slip something ready-made into the microwave?" The answer, I believe, was "hospitality." It was something she could do to live a beautiful life in a fallen world.

Beautiful Word: *Come*

The New Testament ends with an invitation: "Let the one who is thirsty come; and let the one who wishes take the free gift of the water of life" (Revelation 22:17). The Lord is calling, "Come" to all people.

Matt Chandler, a pastor in Texas, tells of being in a meeting for teens where the topic is sexual purity. The speaker asks the audience to pass around a rose and to sniff its fragrance and touch the silky petals. When he finishes his talk, he holds up the crushed, mangled, roughly used rose and asks with disdain, "Who would want this rose now?" Matt said he wanted to stand up and yell, "Jesus. Jesus wants the rose."

It's true. His welcoming invitation extends to the bruised and weakly burning soul, to the ravaged and lonely. "A bruised reed he will not break, and a smoldering wick he will not snuff out" (Isaiah 42:3). His invitation stands: "Come."

> Lord, please reveal anything in my life that might keep others from coming to You. Deal with the Pharisee in me. I want to live a welcoming life like Yours. For the rest of my life, I want to live in the light of "Come."

CHAPTER 17

LIFELONG LEARNER: IF NOT NOW, WHEN?

I want to be a lifelong learner. A follower of Christ must subscribe to this desire. Disciple means learner. If I am His disciple, new vistas open before me. The floor and ceiling disappear. Walls are blown out. A lifetime is too meager a window to learn Christ and the mysteries of the gospel. I know this better now than when I first began.

When the Father hid my life in Christ all those many years ago, He opened a door previously unimaginable. Learning Christ is like standing at a convergence of paths. He is *the* Path: *the* Way, *the* Life, and *the* Truth. Once on His path, beckoning trails radiate out from Him in every direction. Each one has its own appeal and is an invitation to know the Lord Jesus Christ in another circumstance of life. One path leads up a steep hill; another moves me across a broad meadow; another seems to dead-end at the lip of a cliff overlooking a vast and thundering ocean. Paths disappear over a knoll or wind behind an outcropping. Even the one into the gloomy forest, which hints of danger, has its own appeal. Always the path goes farther, opens to new horizons, fresh discoveries, deeper heart-attachments to Christ. All along the way, other paths intersect—inviting, promising worthwhile side trips. On every path, God calls me to live not by what I perceive but by what He reveals. On this journey, seeing is not believing; believing is seeing.

Learning from Me

I believe all this. My Phase 1 adventure is to learn Christ, to know Him, to believe Him, to walk through life with Him. So His invitation is my bridge: "Come to me, all you who are weary and burdened, and I will give you rest. Take my yoke upon you and learn from me, for I am gentle and humble in heart, and you will find rest for your souls" (Matthew 11:28-29).

I was stunned and thrilled to find that the preposition *from* varies in other translations. "Learn *from* me" in the NIV becomes "learn *of* Me" (AMP) or "walk *with* me and work *with* me" (MSG). The obvious constant is Jesus. He calls me to come and learn from Him, of Him, and with Him in all of life. This is a pursuit that cannot disappoint or be exhausted. In the words of David, who knew well that endless delights await those who love God and His life-giving Word, "You make known to me the path of life; you will fill me with joy in your presence, with eternal pleasures at your right hand" (Psalm 16:11).

Jesus as Learner

The boy-Jesus sat among the teachers in the temple asking questions (see Luke 2:42-52). A learner asks questions. A learner benefits from the scholarship and experience of others. I love the Lord for coming to earth as a learner. He is God from eternity to eternity—almighty, all-knowing—yet He came to earth, emptied of His prerogatives as God, to live among us as one of us. He came as one who grows, as one who learns: "Jesus grew in wisdom and stature, and in favor with God and man" (verse 52).

Throughout His life on earth, Jesus noticed the physical world around Him: the farmer sowing in a field, the birds lighting on a mustard plant. Everyday objects and occurrences were windows into spiritual truths. With a sharp eye for natural revelations, Jesus challenged His disciples to "Learn this lesson from the fig tree" (Matthew 24:32). The world system loses its attraction, but as I learn Christ, the created world around me takes on new hues and dimensions. Fireflies and dragonflies, hollyhocks and corn shocks, starlight and firelight all enrich my joy in the Creator. All of life can be contemplated with value.

> Lord, please heighten my awareness and appreciation; make me more alert and receptive to ways the Spirit might illumine the Truth through the world around me.

Learning Obedience

It is one thing to see Jesus learning as a boy or using the physical world to illustrate greater truths, but I am most deeply moved by the learning He was still doing at the end of His life. Jesus "learned obedience from what he suffered" (Hebrews 5:8). What kind of learning is that? Is this the path that disappears into the dark forest? Undoubtedly this learning touches the marrow of His being. It is one thing to engage in "mind-learning," to sit under teachers and ask questions to gain understanding or to learn from observing in the natural world; it is altogether different to learn obedience from what we suffer. No one wants to enroll in the school of suffering. Nevertheless, no one escapes the course. Will I learn obedience in the process? Will I learn Jesus and trust and obey as He did?

Jesus' example of learning obedience sets the bar for me. It isn't enough to grow in knowledge. All my learning must move me into the realm of personal obedience. Will my learning be a translation of biblical truth, a growing conformity to the will of God? Will I, like Jesus, allow suffering to teach me? I struggle with the word order: Will

I embrace the will of God and learn from Jesus, or will I learn from Jesus and embrace the will of God? Both, I hope. That is my "intended wing."

Love of Learning

When friends questioned a man's decision to pursue the study of Greek in his eighties, he responded, "If not now, when?" When, indeed?

The truth is that a love of learning isn't something most people develop in old age. Most often, older learners are continuing in the direction of a lifetime. But I've noticed that when someone comes into vital connection with Christ, at any age, his or her mind comes alive along with his or her spirit. A disciple doesn't need to manufacture an interest to pursue. In Christ dwell all the riches of wisdom and knowledge.

"Oh, the depth of the riches of the wisdom and knowledge of God! How unsearchable his judgments, and his paths beyond tracing out!" (Romans 11:33).

Learn Him.

Father in heaven, enlarge and ready me to learn of Jesus, from Jesus, and with Jesus for the rest of my life. Grace me to learn in good times and hard times, in times of clarity and in times of confusion, in times of gain and in times of loss. Deliver me from "Why me?" to a spirit of "What do You want me to learn about You, from You, and with You?" Bless me to trust You when the lessons seem gauzy and obscure. Even on the trip through the dark forest, grace me with deeper joys of learning You.

CHAPTER 18

LOOKING FOR FRUIT

As I think about my life on earth, the brevity of it, the meaning and purpose of it, questions arise. When I die and see the Lord face-to-face, when the fog of earth and sin no longer cloud my vision, what clarity will confront me? Will I regret, then, that I missed God's revealed will for Phase 1? Will I stand before Him fruitless, a bare, dry branch, instead of one who brings Him glory? What is God expecting from my life?

Two passages in Matthew 21 answer that question for me. In one (see verses 18-22), Jesus was hungry and approached a fig tree expectantly but found no fruit. Jesus cursed the tree and it withered immediately. I wondered, *What's going on here? Was Jesus succumbing to a surly mood?* No. Nor was Jesus trying to awe His friends with an impressive show of power. He was making a point in a dramatic fashion. God expects to find fruit in His people.

The fig tree refers to Israel, the nation God chose and assigned the privilege of revealing Him to the nations. Throughout the Old Testament, God uses imagery of fruit-bearing plants when speaking of His people. Jesus' response to the fruitless fig tree illustrates how severely God responds to fruitlessness.

The Lord places another passage about fruitfulness, a parable, in the same chapter for emphasis (see verses 33-46). The master sends servants to collect his share of the fruit from tenant farmers, but the tenants abuse and kill those he sends, even killing the master's son. The parable concludes with Jesus saying, "Therefore I tell you that the kingdom of God will be taken away from you and given to a people who will produce its fruit" (verse 43).

The message is clear: God rightfully and logically expects fruit. God desires it, expects it, and requires it. Because the nation of Israel failed to produce fruit, God transferred the fruit-bearing privilege and responsibility to those who draw their lives from the Lord Jesus Christ: His church. But as truly as God desires, expects, and requires fruit, it is not the goal; it is the by-product.

What Is This Fruit?

Fruit is a broad-spectrum reality. It is the *observable evidence* of Christ expressing His life in me and through me. It is the fruit of character that the Holy Spirit produces in my life, the life of God incarnated in me reflecting glory back to the Father. It is His life in me to touch others for their salvation and sanctification.

> Spirit of God, fill me, flood me, with Your holy activity. Swell. Overflow. Produce Your bright and burning fruit in me.

Fruit is observable.

An atheistic professor agreed to attend meetings where a Christian apologist was speaking. She was impressed with his presentation but commented that she'd be interested to know what he's like at home. She is right. When someone speaks as one belonging to Christ, there should be evidence in the personal life. When my message and my life are congruous and harmonious, God is glorified. Paul's letters call believers to live lives worthy of the Lord so that the gospel is not maligned (see Titus 2:5; Colossians 1:10). When the world doesn't see appropriate fruit in God's people, the Lord is dishonored and the gospel hindered.

> Lord God, I confess again areas inconsistent with Your character and purposes, unholy and untransformed patterns and well-worn, dishonoring ruts. Produce Your beautiful fruit in me.

Fruit is evidence.

Is there enough evidence to convict me of being a Christian? When others look at my life do they find grounds to support my claim that Christ lives in me? What evidence should they be able to observe? Paul gives a good starter list: "The fruit of the Spirit is love, joy, peace, forbearance, kindness, goodness, faithfulness, gentleness and self-control" (Galatians 5:22-23).

God is looking for fruit; so is everyone else. This fruit is the observable evidence of a mystery: God is resident in me. Clearly, if I live in God and He lives in me, I should bear fruit. How could I not? Unfortunately, many hungry people become disillusioned and cynical when they don't find appropriate fruit in those who profess Christ. Even unbelievers know that if I claim to follow Christ, there should be sweet fruit dangling from my life. Fruit indicates and identifies. An apple tree produces apples. Firm, delicious apples come from healthy apple trees. Nothing is a more certain indicator of the identity and condition of a tree than careful inspection of the fruit.

> Oh, Lord, is there sufficient evidence in my life of Your activity? Will others at least be tempted to speculate whether God ever inhabits humans? I long for the bursting forth of Your life in me that spills over to touch others in blessing, to Your glory. Bear Your fruit in me.

Paul prays for the Philippians that their "love may abound more and more in knowledge and depth of insight, so that [they] may be able to discern what is best and may be pure and blameless for the day of Christ, filled with the fruit of righteousness that comes through Jesus Christ—to the glory and praise of God" (Philippians 1:9-11). The fruit of righteousness is not about being a good citizen, or living by high ideals, or even striving to be a good Christian; the fruit of righteousness is the observable evidence of the life of God in the soul of man. This is a life like no other—abundant life (see John 10:10). This is the Holy Spirit's reign inside a believer welling up into an eternal spring, Jesus' life flowing into a thirsty world.

Sometimes when I consider this, I remember the account of a Sunday school teacher who asked a boy in her class if he wanted to pray and invite Jesus to live in his heart. The boy said it wouldn't work; he was small and Jesus was big and Jesus would stick out all over.

This is exactly the point: Jesus wants to live in me and stick out all over.

Unfortunately, I fear that often Jesus doesn't stick out of my life. How many times have I squelched the life of Christ in me? Disobedience and unbelief are often nearly synonymous in the Scriptures. Both curtail the flow.

Father God, please make me aware of the ways I hinder the expression of Your life in me and through me that I might confess it and repent. I can't produce the fruit You're looking for. Your Spirit must well up in me. Lord, invade every corner and dissolve the distance between what I say and what I do. Even more, dissolve the distance between what I say I believe and what is happening in my heart and mind. Would You so work in me that on the day of the great and final harvest, I will bow before You fully ripened and ready. When I stand before You on my last day on earth, I desire to stand in grateful awe that You answered this prayer, for Your glory and the advancement of Your kingdom. In Jesus' name.

CHAPTER 19

FRUITFUL EVERY SEASON

Blessed is the one who trusts in the LORD, whose confidence is in him. They will be like a tree planted by the water that sends out its roots by the stream. It does not fear when heat comes; its leaves are always green. It has no worries in a year of drought and never fails to bear fruit.

JEREMIAH 17:7-8

Helene Ashker was eighty years old and dying. Over the years, she influenced many women to faith in Christ. Her manner was winsome, whisper-quiet, and invariably direct. Now, after years of conference speaking, leading small groups, teaching women to study the Bible, boldly sharing the gospel, she was homebound, tethered to an oxygen tank. Several times a week, a home health-care worker attended Helene's practical needs. The worker's tasks never required the full four hours, so Helene taught her the Bible. Life narrowed and strength ebbed, but Helene's long fruitfulness was not over.

It doesn't surprise me that Jesus reached out to this health-care worker through a weak and dying woman. In the greatest chapter on fruitfulness in the Bible (see John 15), Jesus says that He expects fruit bearing from tender and easily broken branches. Jesus is the Vine and we are the branches. The Greek word for *branches* comes from the root to break and communicates the idea of tender and easily broken. What rocks my equilibrium is that God produces fruit from these fragile appendages.

> Lord, whatever my age or condition, produce Your fruit in and through me. Weakness is not an excuse or a disqualification. Express Yourself in and through me; grow Your fruit in me to the end.

Jesus is the Vine; His Father is the gardener; we are the branches. The Father trims off fruitless branches and prunes fruit-producing branches for greater fruitfulness. Fruit—the Father tends the plant because He wants fruit. He expects fruit. But Jesus makes it clear that no branch bears fruit unless it is vitally attached to Him. It's God-life surging through, nourishing, vitalizing tender and easily broken branches, that produces [God-life produces] the fruit God desires: "I am the vine; you are the branches. If you remain in me and I in you, you will bear much fruit; apart from me you can do nothing" (John 15:5).

For years, I pondered the question "What does it mean to remain in Jesus?" Various translations express it "abide in" or "dwell in" or "grow in" or "stay in union." Taken together, all are homey words. I conjure up a picture of settling in, unpacking my bags, putting on the kettle, and inhabiting Christ for the duration. These domestic images make the proposition no less mysterious and astounding. Jesus invites me to make my home in Him. At the same time, Jesus and the Father propose making *Their* home in me: "Anyone who loves me will obey my teaching. My Father will love them, and we will come to them and make our home with them" (14:23). This melding, God in me and I in Him, is abiding. This image is imbued with residential pleasure and wonder. Abiding is essential to fruitful living.

Father, You expect fruit and I want to be fruitful. As I look to the rest of my life, what truths, what preparations, what disciplines, what attitudes, what surrenders will enable me to live attached all my life? Live fully in me. Teach and train me to live fully in You.

God in me; I in Him — a marvel. Then He adds another strand to the intimate entwining: "If you remain in me and my words remain in you, ask whatever you wish, and it will be done for you. This is to my Father's glory, that you bear much fruit, showing yourselves to be my disciples" (John 15:7-8). God will live in me, His words will live in me, and I will bear fruit to God's glory. His Word, warm sap rising in tender and easily broken branches, pulses life through and through, buds sweet fruit into existence.

"*If* . . . my words remain in you" — if— "ask whatever you wish, and it will be given you." Ask anything of the Father. G. Campbell Morgan said that *ask* here in the Greek is to "demand as my due."[1] God invites me to ask anything under the condition that I live connected to Him, abiding in Him, remaining in Him, living attached, drawing on His life, bending to His will, allowing His life to flow through me to overflow in fruit. My request, my "demand," evolves from Christ's life flowing in me. My request will be what Jesus would ask. I will ask for "as my due" God's working in and through me to produce much fruit for His glory.

Have I neglected this amazing promise, thinking that bold asking is presumptuous? Jesus invites me to ask. I can glorify God by being more fruitful than I dared to dream. In those times when I feel particularly weak or laid aside, I will nest in Jesus. I will ask Him to shape me to His will and use me and use me and use me. I will remind myself that fruitfulness is God's will for me even when I'm at my lowest. Jesus said so: "You did not choose me, but I chose you and appointed you so that you might go and bear fruit — fruit that will last — and so that whatever you ask in my name the Father will give you" (verse 16).

Am I living attached to the Vine? Am I feeding off His Word, allowing it to nourish and empower my life? Am I applying what I read, taking steps of obedience to conform my life to God's will? Am I believing God, trusting Him? Am I asking God for fruit and more fruit, continual fruit, a lifetime of fruit bearing? Am I asking for others as well, fruitfulness to the end, down to the wire, when we enter into God's presence in glory?

Fruitful to the End

Fruitfulness in every season requires flexibility. The vision must be broad enough, deep enough, to transfer to my changing circumstance. This requires a strong and steady vision, one that plays out all the way to the end. My vision can't be teaching Sunday school or ministering to college students. The time may come when doing those things are impossible, but I can love God and love people to the grave and beyond.

I can do this in every relationship no matter where I am, whatever the circumstance of my life. I can abide in Christ and be a link in the chain to help others know and follow Him. Whether it is in intense, close relationships or brief glancing contacts with people or through prayer, I can seek to glorify God and further His kingdom.

I find the proposition of a fruitful life alluring and compelling. Something inside me rises when I read verses on fruitful living. This was God's design when He made humans and put them in the Garden of Eden. His word to them and to me: Be fruitful. From the beginning of time to the end of a life, God is glorified by fruitfulness. The psalmist sang, "They will still bear fruit in old age, they will stay fresh and green" (Psalm 92:14). So be it.

Father in heaven, may the Lord Jesus Christ express His life more fully to me and through me for Your glory. Make every kind of good fruit erupt from my life to bless the world (see

Matthew 5:16). Would You use me in quiet ways and audacious ways so that it is evident it is *You* working Your life out in me? Even in my greatest weakness, produce Your fruit in my character, conduct, and words. Flow through this fragile branch. Please, for Jesus' sake.

CHAPTER 20

BEE TREE: INVESTING IN FOREVER

He is the one we proclaim, admonishing and teaching everyone with all wisdom, so that we may present everyone fully mature in Christ. To this end I strenuously contend with all the energy Christ so powerfully works in me.

I pass a massive cottonwood on my walks. It would take three people, arms outstretched, reaching to link hands, to encircle its craggy circumference. Except in winter, the tree hums. Honeybees, legs heavy laden with pollen, bobbing at the entrance, wait their turn to enter the hive. Whenever I pass this tree or think of it in my mind, I pray, *God, please let me enter heaven like these bees enter that honey tree, heavy with fruit to Your glory.*

The apostle Paul expressed a similar desire when he spoke of having "a harvest among" the Gentiles (Romans 1:13). I love the harvest image, a full ingathering, ripe, swelling with life, entering heaven with Paul. He wanted Phase 1 to count for God's glory. Paul desired to make a harvest offering to Christ, the fruit of his labors, mature followers of Christ, so sorrow and frustration tinge Paul's letters; he grieved when believers remained "mere infants in Christ" (1 Corinthians 3:1). Paul feared running his race in vain, coming to the hive of heaven with little to show for his labor.

I used to think the godly attitude was to serve Christ and leave the results to Him. It is true that I can do nothing to effect a spiritual result in another (or in myself, for that matter). But when I consider Paul's passion to present mature believers to Christ, I wonder if my attitude isn't too passive, a subtle cop-out. Paul endured great hardship to bring the gospel and build believers sound in doctrine and practice. Paul's letters are full of heart and ache and sweat and tears. I feel the pang as Paul wrote, "My dear children, for whom I am again in the pains of childbirth until Christ is formed in you, how I wish I could be with you now and change my tone, because I am perplexed about you" (Galatians 4:19-20). Paul was perplexed and pained. Why were they not living in the freedom and joy Christ offers? Paul made it clear: God intended more for them than just squeaking through the turnstile at heaven's gate.

Paul wrote, "We proclaim Him, admonishing every man and teaching every man with all wisdom, so that we may present every man complete in Christ. For this purpose also I labor, striving according to His power, which mightily works within me" (Colossians 1:28-29, NASB).

I love this verse. Several times I've chosen it as my verse for the year. I've turned it slowly in meditation, looked at the backside of it, chewed on it, and marinated in it. I've scrutinized a word at a time. When I memorized it, I switched the word order to "Him we proclaim" to reinforce that it is all about Christ. Every time I said the verse with my voice or in my mind and heart, I wanted to feel the weight of His Person as the motivation, power source, and content of my work. *Him.*

"We" reminds me that *my work* for Christ is part of a mighty whole. I may be a hair follicle, or even a bit of dandruff, in the body of Christ, but my contribution is important. So is yours. But neither of us can function as independent agents. "We" means that I, along with you, have a *part* in accomplishing the work of Christ on earth. I must operate not only attached to Christ but also in the context of the greater body of believers. No matter how deeply I invest in another, he or she needs the influence of other believers to reach full maturity.

I pass the bee tree nearly every day and pray.

Paul prayed, labored, and struggled to present to Christ mature believers, believers manifesting Christ's life-transforming beauty. Another letter, the same goal: "Until we all reach unity in the faith and in the knowledge of the Son of God and become mature, attaining to the whole measure of the fullness of Christ" (Ephesians 4:13).

A Work That Lasts Forever

Leonardo da Vinci wrote, "Shun those studies in which the work that results dies with the worker."[1] Although Leonardo was probably thinking about leaving behind a piece of art or architecture, God calls me not only to store up treasure in heaven, but also to leave some treasure behind. The treasure, of course, is *people*—people being made complete in Christ: "What is our hope, our joy, or the crown in which we will glory in the presence of our Lord Jesus when he comes? Is it not you? Indeed, you are our glory and joy" (1 Thessalonians 2:19-20).

Paul ran his leg of the race ever mindful of the generations that follow. Sweat and tears bead and glitter on the pages of Paul's letters. He knew that the kingdom advances only in Phase 1. The clock was ticking, so he labored with all God's surging energy to present everyone mature in Christ. Paul labored and prepared to pass the baton.

I hear the same passion in Peter's letters:

I will always remind you of these things, even though you know them and are firmly established in the truth you now have. I think it is right to refresh your memory as long as I live in the tent of this body, because I know that I will soon put it aside, as our Lord Jesus Christ has made clear to me. And I will make every effort to see that after my departure you will always be able to remember these things. (2 Peter 1:12-15)

Like Paul and Peter, David expressed a sense of responsibility to testify to the generations behind him: "Even when I am old and gray, do not forsake me, my God, till I declare your power to the next generation, your mighty acts to all who are to come" (Psalm 71:18). At every age and stage of life, this is the Christian's calling: engaging to help others come to full maturity in Christ.

Even in great age and frailty, may I bestow some faith-nourishing morsel on the young. Please, Lord, use me to help others become mature laborers for Your kingdom. Like with Paul, Peter, and David, grace me to invest in forever.

Last night, as a friend contrasted two elderly women, one word was repeated: *invest*. One woman, she said, never invested herself in anyone or anything. Her life, shrunk and shriveled, had no point, no focus. She never even doted on her grandchildren. Now, as her life winds to the end, she leaves nothing behind to bless the generation that remains.

Perhaps prayer is my surest investment in future generations. Over the years, my most frequent request has been that all my children and their spouses and all their children and their spouses and all their children and their spouses, generation after generation, until Jesus comes again, will love and serve the Lord. And not only those who come from me physically but also those I touch spiritually. May it be. May the bee tree hum generation after generation.

Father, the redeemed are the treasure that populates heaven to Your glory. Please use me. Make gospel connections

between me and others so I might add some to that glorious
hoard of people — from every tongue, tribe, language,
race — who will bring You glory when we stand before You,
redeemed, in heaven. Please express Your life through me that
I might have a part in bringing honey to the hive of heaven.

CHAPTER 21

RAISED VEINS: THE BODY'S MINISTRY TO ME

I was in my late forties when a neighbor child, sitting with me on the porch steps, said, "You have hands like my grandmother." I thought back to my only memory of my paternal grandmother—her hands bony and pale with bulging, dark veins—and I felt vaguely insulted. Now, at seventy, I see my hands on the keyboard with raised veins, vital lifelines to my heart, and bless them for their work. *Thank You, Lord, for my body and these veins.*

The human body is the gift that's hard to ignore. It constantly and insistently reminds me of its needs: Feed me. Rest me. Bathe me. Protect me. On and on. All of life bends to the body if I permit it. I can't get away from my body, yet some religions seek to deny the body, to live disconnected from it. At the other end, modern secular culture makes the body a "god" to be worshipped, lifted, tucked, injected, suctioned, and supplemented. The tendency is either to spend irrational amounts of time, effort, and money to sustain and improve it or to fail to honor this amazing gift.

When God created humans, He gave us bodies. I am made in the image of God (see Genesis 1:27), who is Spirit. I am a spiritual being with a body; I am a soul with a body. God said this is good (see verse 31). Then, in an unthinkable flip-flop, Jesus was made in *my* likeness (see Philippians 2:7; Hebrews 2:14-17), coming to earth with a body. Jesus said, "Sacrifice and offering you did not desire, but a body you prepared for me; with burnt offerings and sin offerings you were not pleased. Then I said, 'Here I am—it is written about me in the scroll—I have come to do your will, my God'" (Hebrews 10:5-7). The gospel required a body to be given, a body like the human creation He would die for.

The apostle Paul began a premier chapter on the body "I want to remind you of the gospel" (1 Corinthians 15:1). Then Paul summarized and substantiated the gospel: Christ died for our sins; He was buried, raised from the dead, seen by many in His resurrection body. Paul reminds us that the gospel and the body are powerfully intertwined. The Father prepared a *body* for Jesus so He could die for us, so His body could rise from the dead, so He in resurrection flesh could be the first of many to live forever in a resurrected body (see 1 Corinthians 15:20-23).

A new, glorious-forever body will replace this temporary wonder. It's amazing that God lavishes so much attention to detail in a body that won't last, but He does that everywhere: in that tiny, delicate, finely veined alpine flower that quivers in the mountain chill and then fades and dies, as well as in my body. I am a wonder! The psalmist agrees:

> You created my inmost being;
>> you knit me together in my mother's womb.
> I praise you because I am fearfully and wonderfully made;
>> your works are wonderful,
>> I know that full well. (Psalm 139:13-14)

I am watching my amazing body slip into decline. Just as the gravity of living in a fallen world weighs down the spirit, earth's gravity exerts its pressure to unhinge the body. I watch and realize that my body is ministering to me in its limitations and idiosyncrasies. My bulging veins, my thinning skin, and my thickening torso remind me that I am surely moving toward death and a new body. I thank God for the reminder. This world is so seductive; I quickly lose sight of the end. But my faithful body reminds me, tapping me on the shoulder and sometimes kicking me in the shins to whisper or scream that I am weak or I am tired or I am hurting or I am dying. Even in the exultant exuberance of peak health and performance, fatigue after exertion or a speck in the eye quickly destroys any illusion of invulnerability.

The Bible says that this body is but a *seed*, a seed sown in the ground that produces something altogether different from that seed: a resurrection body: "The body that is sown is perishable, it is raised imperishable; it is sown in dishonor, it is raised in glory; it is sown in weakness, it is raised in power; it is sown a natural body, it is raised a spiritual body" (1 Corinthians 15:42-44). I look at my body and marvel at the seed that will be planted at my death. The words that describe my future body—imperishable, glorious, powerful, and spiritual—excite my meditation, and my appreciation for this perishable seed grows. My current body, like Adam's, came from the earth; my new body, like Jesus', comes from heaven (see verses 45-47).

My body is a jar of clay holding a treasure (see 2 Corinthians 4:7). The incongruity of treasure residing in a common pot thrills, especially if I'm the pot and the Holy Spirit is the treasure. In *Holy the Firm*, Annie Dillard wrote, "All day long I feel created. I can see the blown dust on the back of my hand, the tiny trapezoids of chipped clay, moistened and breathed alive."[1] I look at my hand and feel created too. I observe my hand, the skin like dried clay, all veined in cracks—my body, the work of the Potter, a clay pot with the breath of God inside. That God comes to live in most-unlikely me elevates this jar of clay. The clay pot becomes a temple: "Don't you know that you yourselves are God's temple and that God's Spirit dwells in your midst?" (1 Corinthians 3:16). The Holy Spirit's presence in His people exalts and dignifies the lowly pot. His indwelling presence means that my body is not my own; Christ has bought me at great price (see 6:20). My body belongs to the Lord.

My body is a tent, a temporary dwelling, portable, suitable for a pilgrim (see 2 Corinthians 5:1). Once I traced the travels of Abraham and Sarah and pictured them pulling up stakes again and again, camping out year after year. God commended Abraham for his pilgrim attitude: "By faith he made his home in the promised land like a stranger in a foreign country; he lived in tents . . . for he was looking forward to the city with foundations, whose architect and builder is God" (Hebrews 11:9-10). I read those verses and feel my tent swaying in the wind and know that one day it will collapse in a heap. This rickety tent will be replaced with my forever body. Glory!

My body is a seed, a jar of clay, and a tent. Each image speaks of limitation, vulnerability, fragility, and transience. One day the seed will be planted in the earth, the pot will crumble, and the tent will fold. It is in this weakness that my body ministers to me. Built into life on earth is a faithful reminder that I am weak and this body will die. For the believer in Christ, the gloom of the pronouncement is more than compensated for in the truth that when I am released from this earthly body, I will receive a heavenly body (see 2 Corinthians 5:1-5): "Now the one who has fashioned us for this very purpose is God, who has given us the Spirit as a deposit, guaranteeing what is to come" (verse 5). The word picture in the Greek is that the Spirit indwelling is the "earnest money" and "engagement ring" assuring me of my secure and glorious future.

I forget the most amazing things. God gives me a body, and I'm reminded to *rely* on God in my weakness: "We were under great pressure, far beyond our ability to endure, so that we despaired of life itself. Indeed, we felt we had received the sentence of death. But this happened that we might not rely on ourselves but on God, who raises the dead" (1:8-9).

Father in heaven, thank You for giving me a perishable body to remind me that earth is not my home, that this body is frail by design, that I need to rely on You for grace, that this body will die, that my eternal body will clothe me forever. I offer my body as a vessel for Your use and habitation. I offer my clay-like hands for Your service. One day I will leave this tent behind and be clothed with my heavenly dwelling. My mortality will be swallowed by immortality. All praise to God Most High.

CHAPTER 22

WISE REFRAMING: KEEPING MY CORE IN LIFE'S TRANSITIONS

Nor . . . do I now miss the bodily strength of a young man . . . any more than as a young man I missed the strength of a bull or an elephant. You should use what you have, and whatever you may chance to be doing, do it with all your might.

Let there be only a proper husbanding of strength, and let each man proportion his efforts to his powers. Such an one will assuredly not be possessed with any great regret for his loss of strength.

MARCUS TULLIUS CICERO

Three vignettes keep rattling around in my mind, posing questions, bouncing their similarities and dissimilarities against one another. The first vignette comes from a small article I clipped from the Sunday newspaper's magazine: Sylvester Stallone's seventy-year-old mother suffered a heart attack while practicing a trapeze act for Cirque de Soleil. Maybe this is a reasonable choice for her, but it gave me pause.

I envy her the spangly leotard and her athletic ability, but still I wonder.

Second, I thought about Caleb (see Joshua 14:6-14) and his bold pronouncement, "Here I am today, eighty-five years old! I am still as strong today as the day Moses sent me out; I'm just as vigorous to go out to battle now as I was then. Now give me this hill country that the LORD promised me that day. . . . The LORD helping me, I will drive [the Anakites] out just as he said" (Joshua 14:10-12).

Third was a son's observation that as the years passed, his father, an avid gardener, continued his passion in a garden plot that got smaller and smaller until he tended window boxes.

As I think about these true stories of people dealing with aging in the midst of their passions, questions come to mind. What is a healthy attitude? How do I keep a youthful perspective without, foolishly, trying to act young or prove something? What are the issues? What are the guidelines? What attitudes glorify God?

As I've reflected on these questions, I've found the term *wise reframing* helpful. The dictionary lists a bevy of definitions for the word *frame*; many give a good basis for reflection. One led me to think of a picture frame, a supporting structure, an enclosure to improve and enhance. Skillful framers choose the right materials, proportions, and tones, adding to the beauty of the art. Never in history has humanity known the frame better. We live with the TV's rectangular frame, the computer screen, the windshield, and the glowing blue of the cell phone. Athletes must swim within their lane; football players play between the field lines. In poetry, a sonnet must fit within the frame of fourteen lines.

Wordsworth wrote two sonnets *about* sonnets.[1] He wrote of the "sonnet's scanty plot of ground" and of souls "who have felt the weight of too much liberty." Wordsworth mentioned great poets, among them Shakespeare, Petrarch, Dante, and Spenser, who masterfully explored life's deep experiences within the frame, the limiting form of the sonnet. He ended his sonnet considering Milton, who wrote his greatest sonnets *after* he went blind in his forties. Milton himself wrote a sonnet, "On His Blindness," in which he wondered if God "exact(s) day-labour" when He denies "light." Milton concluded that God does not *need* man's works or gifts but that those who "bear his mild yoke . . . serve him best."[2] Is blindness a "mild yoke"? For Milton, it seems so. He continued to produce laudatory poetry within the limiting frame of sightlessness. Similarly, Beethoven composed music though deaf, and Joni Eareckson Tada draws holding a pen in her teeth though paralyzed from the shoulders down.

Reframing means keeping what is important but wisely reconfiguring as necessary. This skill and attitude serves us well at every age. A baby in the family requires major adjustment to schedule and expectation. So does recovery from surgery, a job with increased demands, and a period of unemployment. Maintaining a consistent devotional time often requires reframing when circumstances change. A mother with preschoolers needs to accept that her date with God will probably not look like it did before children. But because God's Word and prayer are essential to a growing and vibrant spiritual life, she is wise to reshape her expectation and practice and not give up altogether. Spiritual disciplines may take a variety of shapes over a lifetime and are worth reframing as long as mental and physical health allows.

I'm a book person. I love to read and study. What if I lose my eyesight? Then, maybe, I will listen to the Bible assisted by the ever-changing technology. What if I lose my hearing, too? Perhaps then I must live mostly in verses I've memorized. What if I lose my memory? Then I will sit in the grace and mercy of God because nothing can separate me from the love of Christ. What if I live in a nursing home? Will I accept new realities and live Christ in them? Will I continue my lifelong passion to know Christ and make Him known there? Will I adapt and adjust without giving up the calling? Will I, by faith, step into perhaps the stiffest challenges of my life without relinquishing my faith and courage? Reframing, like sonnet writing, always requires creativity, humility, and surrender to the imposed limits.

I must live humbly within the limiting realities of my life. As I age, my life may require major reframing. The garden may shrink. Perhaps I will end working in the dark. How do I maintain my core values and motivations as circumstances change? How do I continue in God's call, even if it must take a shape I'd hardly recognize? How do I keep moving toward the goals the Lord has set for me? For me, the irreducible core is to live in union with the Lord Jesus Christ, trusting Him and responding to His call on my life. My part is to cooperate, to live connected to Him that He might express His life through me to bring others to faith and maturity.

Ironman Caleb?

I'm challenged by the example of Caleb, who believed God's promise to him. For forty-five years, that promise invigorated his life. Then at eighty-five years of age, he strained toward the fulfillment, trusting God to go before him and give him victory. Like Caleb, I want to remember that God doesn't rescind His promises or His call because of advanced years. But I don't want to feel the pressure to prove I can do everything I did at forty.

God did something unusual for Caleb: He enlarged his territory in his eighties. For many eighty-five-year-olds, the large garden gives way to a smaller plot, perhaps even a window box. This is a reality that requires acceptance. I admire both Caleb and the passionate gardener for living in the reality God set before them. Caleb lived in the reality of God's promise and strength. The gardener lived in the reality that although his passion for gardening had not diminished, his physical strength had. To quit gardening because he can no longer keep up with a large plot is abdication. He wisely deflects frustration when he draws in the boundaries and continues doing what he loves. I suspect this requires a fair amount of flexibility, adaptability, and creativity as well as a dollop of grounding discernment. It's what it takes to live a sonnet.

It is interesting to note that Caleb, too, was reframing. Caleb promised his daughter in marriage to the man who would conquer the town of Kiriath-sepher. I suspect that Caleb wanted a younger man leading the battle.

Life will expand and contract over our lifetimes. Some things we love may be stripped from us. An ophthalmologist friend retired when he noticed a slight tremor that might have impacted performance of delicate surgeries. For him, reframing wasn't a matter of doing smaller surgeries; it was a matter of passing on his wealth of skills. He taught classes in Africa and left his surgical instruments with a doctor there. Like Moses, he passed the baton to a younger man. The Lord told Moses, "Commission Joshua, and encourage and strengthen him, for he will lead this people across and will cause them to inherit the land that you will see" (Deuteronomy 3:28). Direct leadership was ending. Now Moses' role was encouraging and strengthening.

Many of the examples I've used are not directly tied to the calling Jesus makes upon His disciples to advance His kingdom, but a shrinking garden or a paintbrush held in the teeth brings God glory when the gardener or paralyzed artist seeks to live Christ in changing circumstances. As a follower of Jesus Christ, I must continually readjust to live fruitfully to the end:

> The righteous will flourish like a palm tree,
>   they will grow like a cedar of Lebanon;
> planted in the house of the LORD,
>   they will flourish in the courts of our God.
> They will still bear fruit in old age,
>   they will stay fresh and green,
> proclaiming, "The LORD is upright;
>   he is my Rock, and there is no wickedness in him."
>   (Psalm 92:12-15)

Decreased strength is part of the winding down of life on earth, a reality for most as they age. As for me, I will give up the trapeze and the spangly leotard, embrace the window box, and pray for a portion of Caleb's spirit to believe God and step out in faith. I will live free of the burden to prove I can do everything I did at forty, but I will engage heart and soul as long as any strength remains. The promises age well. I will trust the God of those promises to keep me fresh, green, and fruitful even in old age.

Father God, pour out Your grace on me that I might be supple, pliable, reframeable. Deliver me from the brittleness that keeps me from accepting and flourishing within the frames that expand or contract throughout my life. Grant me the discernment to recognize the changing frame and the grace to respond wisely. Make the transitions of my life places of sweet connection with You. In Jesus' name.

CHAPTER 23

WATCHFULNESS: STAYING AWAKE AND ALIVE

Recently, I lost my credit card and Coffee Trader card. After turning the house inside out and going through all my pockets, I sank down in spirit. I had two free coffees coming to me. But more depressing, I realized that I often zoom around singing in my heart with my mind in neutral. I'm quick and blithe, and too often I come home with a four-cup package of coffee filters when we need the eight-to-twelve-cup size. No question, it is inconvenient when I must return to the store to make the exchange, but the same slack-mindedness in the spiritual realm concerns me more. *Lord God, capture my mind. Make me mindful of You.*

"I keep my eyes always on the LORD. With him at my right hand, I will not be shaken" (Psalm 16:8). When David penned these words, he expressed his desire to live with God fixed in his gaze. These words expressed David's intended wing, but more, this prophetic psalm declares Christ's daily reality. Jesus' mind was always fixed, always conscious of the Father. Every word and decision came under the

Father's direction. Jesus' "mind-fullness" with the intent to obey is the essence of abiding.

I want to abide too, but even my wonder at profound spiritual realities can easily drift into drowsy dullness. The challenge to keep spiritual realities fresh requires a battle stance against a dulling familiarity. Biblical truths sleepily imbibed become a lulling narcotic, an opiate.

> Oh, God, shake me awake. I don't want to merely go through the motions. Make my soul-nerves tingle and vibrate when I read Your Word. Enlarge my capacity to watch over my soul and the souls of others.

"The end of all things is near. Therefore be alert and of sober mind so that you can pray" (1 Peter 4:7). These are perilous times. Deceptions abound (see Mark 13:5-9,18-23).

> Lord, gather me to You that I might stand with You in prayer for the advancement of Your kingdom. Increase in me a holy vigilance to pray against the powers of this world. Your kingdom is a reign of righteousness and truth. Advance this reign in my life, family, church, community. Promote in me a joyous and trembling perception of Your mighty workings in the world. Keep me awake and watchful that I might worship You in spirit and truth. Help me to see with eyes of faith Your activity, even in darkness and upheaval. For Jesus' sake, make me watchful against the enemies of my soul and Your purposes. Awaken me to Your loving and omnipotent presence hovering over this world. Bless me to stand firm in the faith.

In John Bunyan's classic allegory *The Pilgrim's Progress*, Christian and Hopeful, with many trials behind them, reach the Enchanted Ground. Hopeful becomes drowsy and longs for a nap. Christian knows the danger of sleeping here and reminds his traveling companion to "watch and be sober." To stay awake, they engage in hearty conversation. Christian asks questions to keep Hopeful talking. He draws out the details of God's wooing and working in Hopeful's life. Truly, telling our conversion story is a blessed antidote to a groggy spirit. This reminds me that spiritual conversation, starting with where God started with me, keeps me from grave soul dangers.

> Lord, when it is in my power to direct the conversation toward You and Your work in my life, grace me to do it. Remind me not to squander opportunities to fortify myself and others with bracing spiritual conversation.

Keep Awake; I Have an Enemy

If any warning should kick me out of a sleepy-neutral, it's the reminder that a roaring enemy stalks my soul: "Be alert and of sober mind. Your enemy the devil prowls around like a roaring lion looking for someone to devour" (1 Peter 5:8). Self-controlled, sober, clear-headed, not intoxicated with worldly influences, alert, morally perceptive, vigilant against the questionable tentacles creeping under the soul's door. Jesus warned, "Watch and pray so that you will not fall into temptation. The spirit is willing, but the flesh is weak" (Matthew 26:41). I must be ever vigilant against enemies without and enemies within.

Enemies Within

Jesus spoke these words to the church at Sardis:

> I know your deeds; you have a reputation of being alive, but you are dead. Wake up! Strengthen what remains and is about to die, for I have found your deeds unfinished in the sight of my God. Remember, therefore, what you have received and heard;

hold it fast, and repent. But if you do not wake up, I will come like a thief, and you will not know at what time I will come to you. (Revelation 3:1-3)

The church in Sardis looked good. They had a reputation for being alive. But God said their life was ebbing away and was almost gone. God found only a weak pulse and unfinished work. They had not met God's requirements. The city had a reputation for luxury, softness, apathy, and immorality; the church had a reputation for "being alive."

A reputation is a dangerous thing. I've bungled along as a follower of Christ for more than fifty years. I'm much too well thought of in Christian circles. There I have a reputation for being alive. But I ask,

> What, Lord, do You see when You look at me? Are my prayers hollow shells of piety? Does my "spiritual talk" come from fleshly enthusiasm rather than from the Holy Spirit's filling? Oh, Lord God, please don't leave me to myself. I need Your cleansing and filling. Lord, am I a true disciple today? You must assess my state. I'm sure the Sardis church thought they were doing fine. A casual observer might have been impressed. But Your eye penetrates spiritual glitz and convention. Oh, God, I need You. Please don't leave me to myself. Please don't leave me to myself. [repetition intended]

I pray for protection against the weaknesses I know all too well as well as the dangers inherent in the praise of others (see Proverbs 27:21). God calls, "Wake up! Strengthen what remains. Remember, obey and repent." He calls me to watchfulness over my life. He reminds me that reputation isn't a valid indicator of how I'm doing, nor is the praise I receive.

Wake up and repent. Repentance is God's about-face command. This is the military command to reverse direction, decisively, crisply, immediately. Repentance is a necessary bent for my soul's welfare. Psalms resounds with pleas for God to intervene and reveal the heart's condition. It is the equivalent of my frequent prayer "Please don't leave me to myself." Repentance is the response of a watchful life.

> Lord, please enable me to see You as You are and then to see myself as I am. It is only here that I find the needed motivation and content for repentance. I must see You in Your beauty and holiness, Your lovely humility and gracious kindness, to acknowledge the standard for human life. "Shall we all at last attain to the unity inherent in our faith and the knowledge of the Son of God — to mature manhood, measured by nothing less than the full stature of Christ" (Ephesians 4:13, NEB).

Second Coming

"Keep watch, because you do not know on what day your Lord will come" (Matthew 24:42). Contemplating Jesus' second coming stirs me to watchfulness. His parables warn against the dangers of a spiritually sluggish life (see Matthew 25; Mark 13:32-37; Luke 12:35-48). Watching is more than staying awake; it is anticipation and faithfulness. The One my soul loves may come today to gather me to Himself. That hope motivates me to be ready, vigilant and diligent, prepared. I must cultivate a watchful spirit.

> Lord, so many things press in on my attention, things so noisy and demanding. And You quietly linger. How long Your people have waited for Your coming. Lord Jesus, I want to live awake, expectant, my lamp full of oil, faithfully carrying out my duties.

A watchful life is a sentinel, a guard looking back over my shoulder to see if I left my credit card on the counter or dropped it carelessly, a watchman who looks back to see unconfessed sin and an accruing acceptance of spiritual lukewarmness. The sentinel stands guard in the present, too. He asks, "Is your heart still moved by your conversion story? Does the beauty of the Incarnation, the Cross, the Resurrection, and the Glory of the Ascended Christ change everything for you? Are you moved in wonder that God has spoken when you read the Word, or that He lives inside you literally, not figuratively? Are words such as *grace* and *mercy* swelling in sweetness?" Then the sentinel points out into the future. He asks me, "Have you filled your lamp with oil? Are you ready if He comes today?"

CHAPTER 24

TRIPPED UP: DRINK, DRUGS, SEX, MATERIALISM, AND OTHER DANGERS

Sad and scary verses (they're scattered all through the Bible) sometimes stop me cold. Here's one: "As dead flies give perfume a bad smell, so a little folly outweighs wisdom and honor" (Ecclesiastes 10:1). Sad and scary: Even a small and stupid indiscretion can eclipse years of wisdom and honor. A little folly spoils the sweet scent. "Dead flies make the perfumer's sweet ointment turn rancid and ferment; so can a little folly make wisdom lose its worth" (NEB).

This verse is doubly sad to me because Solomon, the man the Lord called the wisest man, wrote it and then let the flies into his life. The flies were already buzzing around Solomon's ointment when the Queen of Sheba traveled a great distance to hear his wise words and see the kingdom wisdom built. Sad, doubly sad, because "as Solomon grew old, his wives turned his heart after other gods, and his heart was not fully devoted to the LORD his God, as the heart of David his father had been" (1 Kings 11:4). The man honored for his wisdom lets in the flies, and something stinks in here.

Of course, Solomon isn't the only one to succumb to sinful folly. A million and one things can trip me up. Living in enemy territory means that I need to maintain a holy watchfulness over my own life. How many times, I wonder, did Jesus caution His followers to watch and pray? "Watch and pray so that you will not fall into temptation. The spirit is willing, but the flesh is weak" (Matthew 26:41). "And lead us not into temptation, but deliver us from the evil one" (6:13).

Jesus warned, "Be careful, or your hearts will be weighed down with carousing, drunkenness and the anxieties of life, and that day will close on you suddenly like a trap. . . . Be always on the watch, and pray that you may be able to escape all that is about to happen, and that you may be able to stand before the Son of Man" (Luke 21:34,36).

Paul reminded the spiritually mature person that soul-dangers are present: "Brothers and sisters, if someone is caught in a sin, you who live by the Spirit should restore that person gently. But watch yourselves, or you also may be tempted" (Galatians 6:1). I take this admonition seriously. I must not let down my guard just because I am older. Now is the time for heightened vigilance. The Bible says that when Solomon was old, when I expect to find his wisdom at apex, foolishness supplanted wisdom and flies polluted the sweet fragrance. More than once I heard my mother say, "There's no fool like an old fool."

Maybe "old" is a sliding scale. Solomon died before his sixtieth year, not an old man by my accounting. Yet the Scriptures say that when he was old, his heart turned to other gods (see 1 Kings 11:4). Is the phrase "as Solomon grew old" a contrast to his early years of obedience and concern for the glory of God, or did dissipation and excess make Solomon "old" before his time? F. W. Farrar suggested in his small volume on Solomon that it "seems to show that the force of his will was much broken by enervating self-indulgence. . . . Sensuality led to religious indifference, and indifference to absorbing worldliness, which ended in the most daring violations of God's most emphatic and express commands."[1]

Solomon flaunted disregard for God's commands to kings (see Deuteronomy 17:16-17), disobeying every one in flamboyant excess. He multiplied horses and wives and plastered gold and silver on every possible surface. Such were the insatiable cravings of this "old man." I consider Solomon's slide away from God and ask, "Father, please show me the things in my life that, unchecked, will trip me up."

Second Timothy 2:21-22 is a good passage for me to consider and pray over: "Those who cleanse themselves from the latter will be instruments for special purposes, made holy, useful to the Master and prepared to do any good work. Flee the evil desires of youth and pursue righteousness, faith, love and peace, along with those who call on the Lord out of a pure heart."

Flies Still Pollute

A woman was surprised and grieved to find her mother, once an active churchwoman, now in a retirement community, drinking Bloody Marys with a friend every morning. Alcohol splashed freely throughout the day. Age doesn't diminish dangers for this woman, or for me. Older men and women still struggle with anger, lust, gossip, overeating, and drunkenness. This is nothing new. Two thousand years ago, Paul warned older men and women against excess in drink (see 1 Timothy 3:2-11; Titus 1:7; 2:3) and called them to vigilance in all of life.

Why might there be a tendency to excess among older people? Perhaps the reasons are no different from those of the college student or the middle-aged. At any age, loneliness, peer pressure, insecurity, guilt, the attempt to dull emotional or physical pain, boredom, plus a host of other roots can lead to alcohol or drug abuse. No one lives long before accumulating a stable of needs and hurts. But loss of direction and purpose—a sense of merely marking time—becomes increasingly debilitating as the finish line looms. With the end in sight and life "going nowhere," the bottle is solace. With my own finish line ahead, I acknowledge my need to continually refocus on the Lord Himself, His calling on my life, His care, guidance, and resources.

Noah, a man of character and faith, let down his guard and let in the flies. After years of trusting God and laboring to build the ark, Noah "became drunk and lay uncovered inside his tent" (Genesis 9:21). Too much wine made Noah unconscious and indiscreet. His nakedness caused shame and disrespect in his sons. A man of honor dishonored himself. "A little folly outweighs wisdom and honor."

> Lord, expose my blind spots, my dulled sensitivities, my drowsy compromises, my dried-out disciplines, my distracting delusions, my unpatched holes. Help me spot the flies, those dark things hiding in the creases of my life. Keep me from the foolish deep-end. Keep me from the slow drift. Guard me against dignified complacency. Lord, please buttress me against letting down my guard at the end.

Age doesn't dampen personal struggle; it often intensifies it. Philip Yancey quotes the French Catholic writer Francois Mauriac regarding the struggle for sexual purity: "Old age risks being a period of redoubled testing because the imagination of an old man is substituted in a horrible way for what nature refuses him."[2]

The big problem from baby steps to the deathbed is self. At every age, at every stage, the looming "I" exerts its gargantuan appetite. I wonder if some view empty-nest freedom as a license for license. The advertising barrage insists that "You deserve a break today" and "This is my time for me." A newspaper ad for a retirement village in Colorado troubled me: "The older we get, the more we want." Devoid of subtlety, it goes on: "*More* choices—*More* Freedom—*More* of everything." That ad, so blatantly self-indulgent and materially minded, made me wonder how I would finish the sentence "The older I get, the more I want . . ." Want what?!

I decided on "the more I want to live responsibly before the generations coming after me." They are watching. Perhaps out of the corner of their eyes, they observe how I handle the freedom of the empty nest and having less mobility, how I use my time and energy, how I discipline my appetite, whether I pursue great truths and virtues or fritter my life away. They see the future in me. They note how I handle life's disappointments, challenges, and the losses that will inevitably come. They watch. Do the promises of God hold up in real life? Can someone live Christ to the very end? Can someone find joy and peace when life strips away amenities?

> Lord, they are watching. Please keep me from follies that spoil the perfume of my life. You call me to exude the sweet aroma of Christ in the world (see 2 Corinthians 2:14-16). I know the tears in the screen door where flies might squeeze into my life. I shudder as I consider all my vulnerabilities and close calls. You know them better, Lord. Grace and mercy, please. Guard my heart. Enlarge in me a spirit of watchfulness, of vigilance, and a sweet and steely zeal. Please, in Jesus' name.

CHAPTER 25

THE LUMP: WHEN FAILURE THREATENS TO OVERWHELM

For years, I lived with an almost palpable "lump." I felt it in my throat and chest, a heaviness I couldn't escape. Sometimes I would groan in the middle of the night and my husband would ask, "Is it the lump?" Every morning, I came to the Lord hopeful that I might make spiritual sense of this anguish lodged in me. I've come to believe that "lumps" can destroy us or bless us, so I've included this personal story. I want to learn the lessons of the lump for the rest of my life.

The lump, a fibrous mass of grief and failure, grew from my failure to love my terminally ill mother as Christ calls me to love. Mired in confusing emotions, I spent weeks at a time on the East Coast caring for Mom, often feeling like a struggling teenager. At one point, I decided that I could continue only if I pretended I was hired help. That's the truth, sad and true; I felt my failure deeply. When I shared my struggle, the lump, and my inability to understand what was going on inside me, several people mentioned Romans 8:1, "Therefore, there is now no condemnation for those who are in Christ Jesus."

It's a great truth, but it didn't touch the issue. I didn't feel condemned. I confessed sin and received God's forgiveness. I sensed no breach in my fellowship with the Lord. Nevertheless, the lump resided, unabated. Before and after my mother's death, I prayed, "Lord, please teach me. What is happening in my heart? What is it You want me to learn, to know, to do?" The Lord revealed Himself day by day, but He didn't speak to the lump.

Then one morning months after Mom's death, He addressed my pain: "Now instead, you ought to forgive and comfort him, so that he will not be overwhelmed by excessive sorrow" (2 Corinthians 2:7). *Lord, is that what's happening to me? Am I being overwhelmed with excessive sorrow?* I knew that God was near and speaking. I sobbed in gratitude.

The word translated "overwhelmed"[1] means to gulp down, to drink entirely, swallow, drown, or devour. The same idea is found in:

- 1 Corinthians 15:54: "Death has been *swallowed* up in victory." *Glory!*
- 2 Corinthians 5:4: "While we are in this tent, we groan and are burdened, because we do not wish to be unclothed but to be clothed instead with our heavenly dwelling, so that what is mortal may be *swallowed* up by life." *Hallelujah!*
- Hebrews 11:29: "By faith the people passed through the Red Sea as on dry land; but when the Egyptians tried to do so, they were *drowned*." *Uh-oh!*
- 1 Peter 5:8: "Your enemy the devil prowls around like a roaring lion looking for someone to *devour*." *Lord, is my sorrow over my sin excessive, and is Satan using it to swallow me up?*

Excessive sorrow over sin goes beyond a healthy repentance and leaves me open to the Enemy. Even sorrow over sin must be capped. Overmuch sorrow puts me in danger of being swallowed up, drowned, or devoured.

Tears flowed. A bit of the lump melted and flowed over the spillway.

I think of Judas taking his own life in unassuaged remorse (see Matthew 27:3-5), devoured. But mostly I think of Peter having "wept bitterly" (Luke 22:62) after he denied the Lord. Etched in Peter's memory: "I don't know Him," the cock's crowing, the Lord's turning and looking straight at Him (see verses 54-62). If anyone could suffer from excessive sorrow, it is Peter. To my relief, the next time I see Peter, he is in the Upper Room with the others, not off nursing the lump in secret (see 24:9). He grieves in their presence. Everybody knows about his failure; all four of the Gospels record the story (see Matthew 26:69-75; Mark 14:66-72; Luke 22:54-62; John 18:15-27). I read these accounts and my lump goes out to Peter. He failed the Lord too.

As I reread the passage, I noticed the phrase "Peter followed at a distance" (Luke 22:54). My heart leaps. Peter was there—following imperfectly, but he was there. I cry again. Even though Peter was terrified and confused, full of self and weakness, he wanted to be near Jesus. He was a stumbling follower. *Me, too, Lord. I sinned, but I was there, desiring to follow You.* Now I weep, not over my sin but in gratitude that God is burrowing into my core with scalpel and balm.

As I track Peter's life, I notice that *before* his denial, Jesus told him that he would fail big but that he should strengthen his brothers when he has turned back (see Luke 22:32). Failure, serious failure, didn't disqualify Peter; perhaps it prepared him to serve the body. Maybe failure does a necessary work. *So, Lord, I place my failure and the painful memory of it at Your service.*

Sifting and Sorrow

"Simon, Simon, Satan has asked to sift all of you as wheat. But I have prayed for you, Simon, that your faith may not fail. And when you have turned back, strengthen your brothers."

But he replied, "Lord, I am ready to go with you to prison and to death."

Jesus answered, "I tell you, Peter, before the rooster crows today, you will deny three times that you know me." (Luke 22:31-34)

It occurs to me this morning that part of my distress may be Satan's sifting. The *you* in verse 31 is plural. The Enemy asks to sift believers.

> Savior and Redeemer, I offer my sinful, selfish attitudes (which are forgiven and cleansed by Jesus on the cross) to You for Your purposes. I place them under Your blood and at Your feet. Redeem my failure and use it to make Satan sorry he sought to sift me. Use my failure to advance Your kingdom like You did for Peter, the cowardly failure who joined other cowardly failures in the Upper Room. You used such to change the world.

Failure is certain. Repentance is required (see 2 Corinthians 7:10). Excessive grief is destructive.

I repented, received forgiveness and cleansing, yet the lump remained. When I read Luke 5:12, I made it my own: "While Jesus was in one of the towns . . ." *Montrose, Lord?* ". . . a man came along who was covered with leprosy" *or a woman, like me, Lord, with a painful memory.* "When [she] saw Jesus, [she] fell with [her] face to the ground and begged him, 'Lord, if you are willing, you can make me clean.'" *Lord, I have received Your forgiveness and cleansing, yet I feel the need of a cleansing that heals conscience and memory. You can heal me if You are willing.*

More than a decade since my mother's death, the lump's intensity has diminished, although I still feel it deeply at times. Is the painful memory a gift, like Jacob's limp, to remind and humble me? David wrote much of God's forgiveness, yet he continued to feel the heaviness of past sins.

Lord, do You allow sorrow over sin to continue to humble us and stir gratitude? Certainly Paul carried the stinging memory of persecuting the church all his life. Lord, I desire to be set free to live fully in cleansed joy. But if You want me to accept the cleansing You have provided without cleansing my memory, give me grace to leave it there. I'm listening.

I read my journals and realize I began grieving my mother's death years before she died. Then, as I cared for her, I grieved what I saw in myself. Now I think of the lump as a wound, mostly clean and tender. I learn from Søren Kierkegaard's wisdom, "in order for the wound to be healed, the wound must be kept open."[2]

Healing the Open Wound

I know this on the physical level. Days after surgery, the doctor opened my husband's incision to extract a blood clot. The doctor left the wound open to heal from the inside out. It was intimate work, dealing with the insides, daily swabbing and packing. The danger, of course, is infection. I must face this roseate slash though I want to turn away. Wound work requires a strong stomach and much grace. I handle the spiritual lump, too, and attend the florid spiritual wound. I know the lump can harm me; I now believe the lump can bless me. The lump reminds me that I am a sinner saved by grace. The wound, mostly healthy and healing, reminds me that I have a Redeemer: "Do not gloat over me, my enemy! Though I have fallen, I will rise. Though I sit in darkness, the LORD will be my light. Because I have sinned against him, I will bear the LORD's wrath, until he pleads my case and upholds my cause. He will bring me out into the light; I will see his righteousness" (Micah 7:8-9).

Lord, I offer the lump and the wound to You. Thank You that in Christ I am more than lump and wound. Thank You that You use all things to reveal Yourself and shape Christ in me. Thank You for forgiveness and cleansing and giving me a future and hope. Thank You that You use failures to build Your kingdom. I'm grateful.

CHAPTER 26

EMBRACING THE CROSS: PREPARING TO DRINK MY CUP

Recently I pulled our Easter scroll down from the top shelf in the closet and unrolled it. The "scroll" is a roll of shelf-lining paper as yellowed with time as ancient parchment, lined off in frames, depicting the last days of Jesus' life in pencil, drawn many years ago by our young children. I wish I knew a way to preserve this decaying treasure from its brittle demise. Our youngest son drew cowboy boots on Jesus and the disciples; this always makes me laugh. But when I get to a particular frame drawn by our daughter, I gasp. Jesus is kneeling by a large rock in Gethsemane; resting atop that rock is His coffee mug. And Jesus is praying, "My Father, if it is possible, may this cup be taken from me. Yet not as I will, but as you will" (Matthew 26:39).

What was this cup, this cup that caused Jesus such wrenching soul distress? I need to know. The Bible makes clear that I, too, have a "cup." *Lord, how do You want me to think about Your cup and mine?*

New Bible Dictionary ends its section on the cup with this: "Throughout the Bible, cup is used figuratively as containing the share of blessings and disasters allotted to a man or nation or his divinely appointed fate."[1] David sang of his delightful cup,

> You prepare a table before me
>   in the presence of my enemies.
> You anoint my head with oil;
>   my cup overflows.
> Surely your goodness and love will follow me
>   all the days of my life,
> and I will dwell in the house of the LORD forever. (Psalm 23:5-6)

The psalmist exulted, "What shall I return to the LORD for all his goodness to me? I will lift up the cup of salvation and call on the name of the LORD. I will fulfill my vows to the LORD in the presence of all his people" (116:12-14). Did he lift the cup of salvation in toast or for filling?

David hoists his cup with joy and gratitude. He exalts in the blessings that fall within the boundaries of his life. Like the frames on our Easter scroll and the frame around David's life, my life has a context. My DNA, the century and geography I'm born into, the opportunities within the range of possibility, and a host of other factors all shape my life. Within this context, the Lord apportions blessings and difficulties, making up my cup.

In the Old Testament, the cup is often an expression of wrath and judgment: "In the hand of the LORD is a cup full of foaming wine mixed with spices; he pours it out, and all the wicked of the earth drink it down to its very dregs" (Psalm 75:8).[2] On the cross, Jesus drank the cup of judgment meant for me. Innocent lips—holy lips—drained the bitter cup. God's righteous judgment rained down in battering blows on the Son. He came to drink the cup I deserve, and drink it He did. "Having drained the cup, He held it up inverted when He said 'It is finished!' and not a drop trickled down the edge. He drank it all that we might never need to drink it."[3] On that night in Gethsemane,

[Jesus] took Peter and the two sons of Zebedee along with him, and he began to be sorrowful and troubled. Then he said to them, "My soul is overwhelmed with sorrow to the point of death. Stay here and keep watch with me."

Going a little farther, he fell with his face to the ground and prayed, "My Father, if it is possible, may this cup be taken from me. Yet not as I will, but as you will." . . .

He went away a second time and prayed, "My Father, if it is not possible for this cup to be taken away unless I drink it, may your will be done."

When he came back, he again found them sleeping, because their eyes were heavy. So he left them and went away once more and prayed the third time, saying the same thing. (Matthew 26:37-39,42-44)

Jesus prayed; the disciples slept. This season of prayer (a night's worth), in intense communion, confronting His horror and revulsion, prepared Jesus to drink His cup, our cup. Soon the betrayer would cut through the black night, come to kiss Him, leading an armed rabble, and Jesus would be ready. Prepared by wrestling and submission, He would face the next hours with settled bedrock strength, fortified by the Father's presence and will.

Violently awakened, dazed, and disoriented, unprepared in every way, the disciples faltered in the terror and confusion. Peter, always ready to do something—anything—sliced through the air and ear of the High Priest's servant. Like a deck chair on the Titanic, slipping toward the precipitous edge, Peter stood in contrast to Jesus, who was prayed up and strengthened and had surrendered to the Father's will. "Jesus commanded Peter, 'Put your sword away! Shall I not drink the cup the Father has given me?'" (John 18:11).

Truly, He would drink the cup. It was the divinely appointed course for His life. Jesus knew the contents of His cup; He had known it for some time. He told His disciples, "The Son of Man will be delivered over to the chief priests and the teachers of the law. They will condemn him to death and will hand him over to the Gentiles to be mocked and flogged and crucified. On the third day he will be raised to life!" (Matthew 20:18-19). Perfection would consume the contents of the foaming and fetid sin-filled cup, the cup filled with my sin.

Would I want to know ahead of time the contents of my cup? That Jesus knew and pondered the coming agony helps me understand the torment of that Gethsemane night. Jesus did not face the Cross lightly, untouched by dread; He lived something of the misery *before* the event itself. This is part of what it means that He shared our humanity.

Earlier, when James and John lobbied for the places of honor in His coming kingdom, Jesus asked,

> "You don't know what you are asking. . . . Can you drink the cup I am going to drink?"
>
> "We can," they answered.
>
> Jesus said to them, "You will indeed drink from my cup, but to sit at my right or left is not for me to grant. These places belong to those for whom they have been prepared by my Father." (verses 22-23)

The disciples had a cup. So do I.

My Cup

So far, I say with David, "LORD, you alone are my portion and my cup; you make my lot secure. The boundary lines have fallen for me in pleasant places; surely I have a delightful inheritance" (Psalm 16:5-6). I believe that the Lord wants me to rejoice in and fully enjoy every pleasant cup. The unknown, difficult cup will not diminish my cup of joy. I don't know what cup awaits within the lines of my story. All I know is that whatever God allows to flow into the frame of my life, it is for my perfecting and His glory. *Lord, help me to receive it in that knowledge and spirit. Your will be done.*

How do I think about this? Is there any way to prepare for my cup? The Lord's entire life was a preparation for His cup. Every surrender to the Father's will readied Him to say in Gethsemane, "Your will be done." Jesus' prayers from the heart prepared Him for the Cross, His cup (see Hebrews 5:7).

The sleeping disciples lacked the benefit of fortifying prayers, but they had eaten the Passover meal with Him just hours before. In ignorance, they had lifted the cup and drunk, the cup that is reminder and preparation. I drink the communion cup and remember that Jesus, in willing obedience, drank the cup of judgment for me, His blood shed for the remission of sin. I lift the cup and drink in gratitude. In this painless remembering and drinking as I sit elbow to elbow with others, God prepares me to drink my cup. Greatest blessing comes to me through the body broken for me and the blood poured out for me. Whatever lies in store for me, my cup, my portion, my story is forever informed and transformed by Jesus' sacrifice. He drank the bitter cup for me. Now as I drink the cup of remembrance, I reflect that the cup of judgment is empty. I reflect too that "the life . . . is in the blood" (Leviticus 17:11). The communion cup affirms and reminds that Jesus lives in me. Because He drank the cup, the life I now live is His life in me. Whatever lies in store for me, I will not be alone when I drink my cup.

CHAPTER 27

GROWING SWEETER THROUGH LIFE'S BITTER TIMES

At the end of a long journey, weariness accumulates. Everyday life itself—step upon step, stress upon stress, day upon day—wears away strength. Like wind and rain that erodes rock little by little, daily life exacts a toll. Resources are depleted. Buffers wear thin. Slights, once brushed off, laid aside to press on with the tasks at hand, now sting deeply as life closes in.

I see this as the apostle Paul expressed his greatest hurts and disappointments in his second letter to Timothy. His end was near, and he knew it: "I am already being poured out like a drink offering, and the time for my departure is near" (4:6). This letter was subdued. An earlier prison letter (Philippians), written while Paul was under house arrest, was buoyant and ecstatic, full of joyful superlatives. But now his weariness shone through. From the grim Mamertine Prison in Rome, a dismal underground dungeon with a hole in the ceiling for light and air, Paul expressed his emotional distress: "You know that everyone in the province of Asia has deserted me, including Phygelus and Hermogenes" (2 Timothy 1:15). Paul mentioned desertions at the beginning and end of this letter (see 4:9). I don't know the details, only that Paul felt the pain intensely.

Yet, even as Paul felt death's foul breath on his neck and the desertion of colaborers in his craw, he held fast to greater truths and callings. Paul continued, as he had for roughly thirty years, to advance the kingdom of God. He urged the young pastor Timothy to guard the gospel (see 1:14) from corrupting doctrines and practices. As the end neared, Paul reminded Timothy—and, I think, himself—to be kind and not resentful in life's bitter times. He wrote, "The Lord's servant must not be quarrelsome but must be kind to everyone, able to teach, not resentful" (2:24).

Not resentful.

Not resentful, but kind.

I suspect that Paul spent some moments in that dank prison hole resisting resentment. His life was "poured out" for the good of the churches and now, in *his* time of need, he experiences feelings of abandonment. Paul wrote that "at my first defense, no one came to my support, but everyone deserted me" (4:16). He faces the end of his life on earth, not surrounded and supported but amid opposition and desertions. This is fertile soil to spawn soul rot and blight. A man must be vigilant in times like these. Life's bitter moments come throughout a life and in varied forms. No one escapes. But I stand in gaping astonishment when I see a "burning bush person" like Paul—someone standing in "flames" but not consumed.

> Father, please hold me fast in tough times. Please keep me from getting completely swamped in the swirling vortex of my pain, forgetting You. Guard me against living solely in my hurts. Give me a vision for all that is greater than my circumstance. Swoop in and hover near.

I look at Paul again. How did he resist soul-withering resentment and bitterness? He resolved to be kind and not resentful to the end. Kind, mild, affable: "We were gentle among you, like a nursing mother taking care of her own children" (1 Thessalonians 2:7, ESV). Kind and not resentful, but forbearing, bearing evil without resentment. Why this high standard?

One, because it is Christlike.

Two, because the advancement of the gospel is greater than our individual lives. The aging apostle, in dire circumstance himself, calls young Timothy to guard the gospel and to guard his own heart and action. The message must not be maligned by the messenger.

Three, because this is the way to know Christ more deeply.

Kind, Like Christ

Suffering comes to all people because we live in a fallen world. The Son of God left heaven's perfection to live in this place of suffering for my sake. He suffered for sins not His own. I will (in a far inferior sense) suffer the consequence of others' sins as well as my own. Peter reminds slaves suffering under an unjust system that Christ suffered unjustly for them:

> To this you were called, because Christ suffered for you, leaving you an example, that you should follow in his steps. . . . When they hurled their insults at him, he did not retaliate; when he suffered, he made no threats. Instead, he entrusted himself to him who judges justly. He himself bore our sins in his body on the tree, so that we might die to sins and live for righteousness; by his wounds you have been healed. (1 Peter 2:21,23-24)

Jesus is my example in suffering. Although everything He suffered was undeserved, resentment did not eat away His insides, nor did He lash out in retaliation. His teaching and practice is radical: "Bless those who persecute you; bless and do not curse" (Romans 12:14).

"Love your enemies and pray for those who persecute you, that you may be children of your Father in heaven" (Matthew 5:44-45). "Father, forgive them, for they do not know what they are doing" (Luke 23:34).

Jesus entrusted Himself to the Father's loving care. He tells me to do the same: "Those who suffer according to God's will should commit themselves to their faithful Creator and continue to do good" (1 Peter 4:19). Trust God and continue to do good. Aaaahh! Now I notice a phrase squeezed in between "kind to everyone" and "not resentful": "able to teach." Even in life's bitter times, the disciple is called to advance God's purposes in the world. Paul taught Timothy in words, but, more powerfully, he taught by example. Paul did not cave in to hurt and disappointment. He did not withdraw to nurse resentment. Instead, he wrote a letter to encourage a young pastor to guard the gospel, to be kind and not resentful, to endure hardship as a good soldier of Christ (see 2 Timothy 2:3). This outward gaze, entrusting oneself to the Father's loving care and seeking to do good, is an antidote to bitterness.

Antidotes to Bitterness

Prison gave Paul time to think, time to replay the injury, the perjury, the injustice done to him. Time. What did he, the consummate missionary, do when his world shrinks down to four slimy, dripping walls? What did a man who walked and sailed all over the Middle East, Europe, and western Asia turning the world upside down do when life closed in on him?

Mostly his options were ones of attitudes, of choosing the path that his mind would travel, of keeping his mind and spirit tethered to Christ, always Christ. Paul followed his own advice and thought on what was true, right, noble, pure, lovely, admirable, excellent, and praiseworthy (see Philippians 4:8). A disciplined mind kept Paul from the easy slide into self-pity and bitterness, debilitating anxiety and self-absorption, soul-saturated rage and despair. A brooding, runaway mind hollows out a man.

Instead, Paul lived in hope. He began this letter by identifying himself as "an apostle of Christ Jesus by the will of God, in keeping with the promise of life that is in Christ Jesus" (2 Timothy 1:1). The promise of life. This hope nourishes and renews:

> We do not lose heart. Though outwardly we are wasting away, yet inwardly we are being renewed day by day. For our light and momentary troubles are achieving for us an eternal glory that far outweighs them all. So we fix our eyes not on what is seen, but on what is unseen. For what is seen is temporary, but what is unseen is eternal. (2 Corinthians 4:16-18)

Called to Suffer

Why is it that suffering takes me by surprise (see 1 Peter 4:12)? I think it is because I was not created to suffer. In God's perfect plan, I was made for garden perfection, but with sin came suffering. God did not *create* me to suffer, but He *calls* me to suffer. He calls me to identify with and participate in His suffering (see verse 13). In this way, I know Him more intimately and experience His powerful working in my life (see Philippians 3:10). Even in life's bitter times, He calls me to have a part in advancing His kingdom.

The Sweet Way

Jean, in times of hurt and disappointment, times when people let you down, remember that Jesus was misunderstood, misrepresented, mistreated, deserted, denied, spit upon, stripped, beaten, and cruci-fied—for you. Remember that hurts can intensify, especially near the end of life. Just at the time you long to have dear ones close, you may feel alone, deserted. But Jesus will stand near you (see 2 Timothy 4:16-17). Remember that things are not always as they seem. Give people and situations the benefit of the doubt. "Deserters," too, are fighting internal battles, just like you are. Resist resentment, and be kind. Guard your heart. When life closes in, what will you believe about God, and what will you believe Him for?

My Father, my Example, my Advocate, loose my soul to see You and delight in You even in life's bitterest times. Remind me, "The LORD himself goes before you and will be with you; he will never leave you nor forsake you. Do not be afraid; do not be discouraged" (Deuteronomy 31:8). Stir me to faith: "The LORD delights in those who fear him, who put their hope in his unfailing love" (Psalm 147:11). Turn my eyes outward to You in worship and to others in kindness. Guard me from soul-fouling sourness. Instead, may I know You in sweet connection, in ways impossible apart from sharing in Your suffering and comfort (see 2 Corinthians 1:5). Amen.

CHAPTER 28

LOSS AND LEAVING

I started drawing when I was a toddler. Pen and paper were a way of life, boxes of drawings accumulated under my bed. My parents took away my sketch pad at a funeral or on a winding road on a car trip. Once I learned to write, I reveled in journals, note-taking, lists of goals, lists of lists. A smooth-writing pen gliding over paper gives me an emotional charge, but not quite on the level with kissing. I feel an immediate kinship with someone bent over a notebook at a back table in a coffee shop. I think solitary confinement might rank just beneath an ocean cruise if the stack of paper and supply of pens were adequate.

My lifelong love affair with pen and paper has not diminished, but I have lost my ability to wield the pen. A few years ago, I developed what is called an intention tremor. The tremor is dormant until I begin to write or butter my bread or chop vegetables. I miss journaling, handwriting thank-you notes, writing grocery lists, and penning peoples' names on my calendar. I miss the ability to take down a phone number or message for my husband or inscribe a book to a friend.

I miss.

Yet it is a small loss, really. It doesn't affect my overall health (which is excellent) or my life span (unless I'm using a knife in the kitchen). Still, it is a loss, one of many that come in a lifetime.

Living with Loss

Life is full of loss and leaving. Mary Nelle was counseled to go back to the places she and her deceased husband had loved and to say good-bye to them. Before she left her home to move to Montrose, she said good-bye to the home she had lived in for many years.

Good-bye is a word that loosens earth's hold on me. Painful as it is, good-bye cuts the cables that release my boat from the harbor and frees me to float closer to my real home. Good-bye reminds me that the idea that I possess anything is illusionary. My dear ones are not mine to have and to hold forever. Earthly relationships are transient. The house we put so much of ourselves into passes from our grasp. The job that identifies us at parties is lost; the skill that was linked with our names diminishes. The loopy cursive becomes a jittery scribble. "Good-bye, dear pen."

I heard on the radio that Pat Summitt, legendary coach of the University of Tennessee Lady Volunteer basketball team, has been diagnosed with early-onset Alzheimer's disease. She has coached there for thirty-eight years and led the team to many championships. Her name is synonymous with women's basketball. What does a woman do when confronting a major loss? Pat said, "It is what it is. What it becomes is what I make it." All of us will live with losses. For us, too, they will become what we make of them.

Losses redirect. Losses force reevaluation and reshaping. Losses plop me down in unfamiliar territory, often without a map. Losses cause me to seek out others who have experienced similar losses. Losses sometimes bring surprising gains.

I think of the Lord's mother losing her reputation to become most blessed among women. When his brothers sold him into slavery, Joseph lost his freedom in order to save many. Paul lost all that he worked so zealously for as a "religious" man—his standing in the community, his vigorous adherence to the Jewish system—lost it all to know, follow, and serve Jesus Christ. As with Mary, Joseph, and many others, Paul's loss came from the hand of the Father. Paul counted this loss as nothing compared with gaining Christ (see Philippians 3:7-9).

Of course, Jesus suffered the greatest loss and leaving, a loss and leaving that we must strain to imagine. He laid aside every privilege and glory as God, left His place in heaven, and pitched His tent in the fallen world. "Being in very nature God, [Jesus] did not consider equality with God something to be used to his own advantage; rather, he made himself nothing by taking the very nature of a servant, being made in human likeness. And being found in appearance as a man, he humbled himself by becoming obedient to death—even death on a cross!" (2:6-8).

Losses take many forms. In God's sovereign plan, loss often comes before a gain. Is emptying a prerequisite to filling? *Father, in Your great mercy help me trust You that there is gain in my losses.*

The Lord Gives and Takes

It seems to me that Job's words are true in ways I've never pondered: "Naked I came from my mother's womb, and naked I will depart. The LORD gave and the LORD has taken away; may the name of the LORD be praised" (Job 1:21).

> Father, You are the Giver-God. All good things come from Your hand. Every breath is bequeathed by grace. "Every good and perfect gift is from above, coming down from the Father of the heavenly lights, who does not change like shifting shadows" (James 1:17). You give and You take away.

The same unchanging Father of lights "takes" with the same love that motivates His giving. There is no darkness in the taking, no shifting shadows. Loss and leaving are part of life. Although I've known loss, I suspect that my greatest losses lie ahead.

The challenge is to live well amid losses and leavings. It isn't easy.

What ripping and wrenching pain to lose a spouse, a child, a close friend. Roger and I were married such a short time when I could no longer determine where he ended and I began. Our lives entwined; over the years the melding intensified. Surely my flesh will tear if he is taken.

Lord, I don't know what losses may drive me to this chapter in the future, but it is "my intended wing," my high desire, to surrender to Your "taking" and gratefully receive what You give. This chapter represents my "advance-work" to prepare my heart for future joys and sorrows. Light my way in loss and gain. Remind me that what You give and take is my biography, a story meant to bless me and bless others to Your glory. If it would glorify You to restore my ability to write with a pen, I ask it. If not, I trust You for the gain that comes with loss.

CHAPTER 29

WIDOWHOOD: WHAT SHAPE WILL MY NEW LIFE TAKE?

Grief, lashed as it is to death, instructs. It teaches that one must invent a way back to life.

KAY REDFIELD JAMISON

A best friend became a widow this year. I pen another name on the "widows' page" in my prayer concerns. I try to put myself in her place, to imagine what she is feeling, needing. Statistics suggest that my name will be included one day on the widows' page. I know that if I lose my husband, I will feel upended.

The Lord reveals Himself as compassionate (see Exodus 34:6), the God of the upended. I'm moved when I read that God is *moved* by my pain and loss: "In all their distress he too was distressed, and the angel of his presence saved them. In his love and mercy he redeemed them; he lifted them up and carried them all the days of old" (Isaiah 63:9). "Though he brings grief, he will show compassion, so great is his unfailing love. For he does not willingly bring affliction or grief to anyone" (Lamentations 3:32-33). I love the tenderness of these words from God.

Widows are vulnerable, and they know it. God knows it too and addresses the vulnerability a woman feels when she loses the leadership and companionship of her husband (see Isaiah 54:4-6). He commits Himself to the widow: "Your Maker is your husband — the LORD Almighty is his name — the Holy One of Israel is your Redeemer; he is called the God of all the earth" (verse 5). God pays special attention to the upended: "A father to the fatherless, a defender of widows, is God in his holy dwelling. God sets the lonely in families" (Psalm 68:5-6). God watches over the widow, orphan, and alien (see 146:9). "Do not take advantage of the widow or the fatherless. If you do and they cry out to me, I will certainly hear their cry. My anger will be aroused" (Exodus 22:22-24). *Lord, You care, You see, You are moved by my pain. Move me to "cry out" to You in my need, assured that You hear.*

Oh, the living power of God's words! His Word flexes and supports the widow in her need like a bungee cord stretching into her grief, allowing her to drop and sag into the loss that is part of life on earth but keeping her from hitting the destroying bottom. His Word, administered by the Holy Spirit, exerts its force, pulling her back into His embrace. His love will not let her go. His very great and very precious promises are the powerful expression and loving tension that keep her to the end for His glory.

In my marriage, Roger often imparts courage to me. "You can do this!" he says. God's Word does the same. The Lord intends that I draw confidence and courage from Him to face life alone. I will learn from other women. "She did it; so can I!" The Lord makes these provisions to impart courage. When I am dismayed, when courage is drained away, my Lord will come to me and strengthen me within. "Do not fear, for I am with you; do not be dismayed, for I am your God. I will strengthen you and help you; I will uphold you with my righteous right hand" (Isaiah 41:10).

After Widowhood

I've noticed recently how often a death is followed, soon after, with the birth of a baby in the family or to someone nearby. Death and birth are the cycle of Phase 1. The arrival of a baby, fresh with the fragrance of heaven, convinces me that there is still much to live for. Author Kay Redfield Jamison said that much is lost with death, but not everything.[1] As she seeked to regain her footing, she wrote, "Each day, each week, I pushed further, thinking to see how much of life I could let back in before having to dart to the safety of sleep or a restless walk"[2]

If I become a widow, Lord, help me accept that life is not over. A life of another substance begins. Lord, what shape will my new life take? I consider some widows God includes in the biblical record. In the Old Testament book of Ruth are the stories of three widows in one family. Each one made choices that mattered to her world. The account reads a little like a fairy tale: three widows, the choice to go or to stay, a journey to a new land, a deeply grieving older widow, a noble young widow, a romance, a rescuing prince, remarriage, and eventually a handsome grandson born to become a king. Although the story has the obligatory happy ending, the grim side is not ignored.

While living in a foreign land, Naomi's husband and two married sons died. The pain of triple loss, understandably, sank her into depression. In her heart, she changed her name from Naomi (Pleasant) to Mara (Bitter). But still something about her (her kindness? her faith? her love for her daughters-in-law?) made her sons' widows want to be with her. One daughter-in-law, Ruth, left her own land to travel with Naomi back to Bethlehem. Together these two widows struck out toward a new life. Naomi provided wise counsel, and Ruth, a woman of faith and character, maneuvered the cultural minefield with vigor and industry. Ruth remarried, became a mother, and the great-grandmother of King David, and one of the four women, besides Mary, mentioned in the genealogy of Jesus. Ruth's first husband died, but her life was not over. Naomi, too, knew great joy as she dandled a "grandson." God blessed these widows and blessed the world through them.

Life was not over for Anna, either, when, after only seven years of marriage, her husband died. The biblical account compressed her life into three packed verses (see Luke 2:36-38). Anna devoted herself to worship, fasting, and prayer. She fellowshipped among those who fervently longed for the Messiah's appearing and was blessed, at eighty-four years of age, to see the yearned for fulfillment: the infant Jesus.

It seems that Mary, our Lord's mother, was a widow by the time Jesus started His public ministry. Scattered throughout the Scriptures are the stories of other widows under God's eye.

> Father in heaven, please lay grace-strokes of preparation in my life so that if I'm a widow, I will courageously seek the shape of my new life under Your direction. Undergird me. Build into my life, in advance, the God-ward intent that will prepare me for whatever is to come.

Stepping Up

Although widows and orphans are among the world's most vulnerable, God sometimes calls them to step out even further on the limb, stretching and building their faith. Daniel and Joseph were essentially orphans called into incredibly challenging circumstances as teenagers. How alone and exposed they must have felt, yet they stepped up and stepped out. They trusted and obeyed God, and He glorified Himself through them. I find it interesting that God used a widow at the end of her rope to minister to the great prophet Elijah.

A drought devastates the land. The brook of Elijah's supply dries up and God chooses to use a starving widow at the end of her resources, both physically and emotionally, to minister to His prophet's needs (see 1 Kings 17). Elijah finds the widow gathering sticks to cook a last meal. Elijah tells her to feed him first and then to fix something for herself and her son (oh, the gall). Most important, Elijah gives her a word from God: "The jar of flour will not be used up and the jug of oil will not run dry until the day the LORD sends rain on the land" (verse 14). A word from God believed and acted upon, and God steps into a desperate situation.

> Lord, You chose a distressed widow to work through. Why? What do You want me to take away from this account? You gave her the privilege of colaboring with You by faith. You exalted her in her humble circumstance to be party to a mighty work. Use me, too. Bless me that I might be a blessing in that hour when all seems lost.

Another widow in distress cried out to another prophet (see 2 Kings 4:1-7). Creditors were threatening to enslave her two sons in payment for debt. In that culture, sons were a widow's security. Elisha asked this poor widow,

> "What do you have in your house?"
>
> "Your servant has nothing there at all," she said, "except a small jar of olive oil." (verse 2)

Then God engaged this woman in a miracle of supply. At Elisha's direction, the widow and her sons borrowed a large number of empty containers from neighbors. Once home, they closed the door and filled those empty jars from their tiny store of oil. They poured and poured. That tiny bit of oil stretched until all the jars were filled. She sold that oil, paid her debts, and lived on what was left.

Stressed resources were a common theme. I remember the widow who captured Jesus' attention by giving her last mite (see Luke 21:2-4). Yet, out of personal need, these widows took care of others. Ironic? No, Christlike. "You know the grace of our Lord Jesus Christ, that though he was rich, yet for your sake he became poor, so that you through his poverty might become rich" (2 Corinthians 8:9).

Father, when I'm upended, help me turn my eyes to You. When my options shrink, help me remember that Your options aren't limited. Grace me to not collapse in on myself but to step into life, trusting You. Please let me serve Your purposes even if I'm emotionally down, stressed, confused, destitute.

Build into my life now the bent of faith that will serve me in the future. Help me to believe that there is still more life to be lived and that You love to use the widow who believes Your Word.

CHAPTER 30

TIME TO BE IN EARNEST

At the age of seventy-seven and possibly facing the onset of Alzheimer's, P. D. James, the acclaimed British mystery writer, agreed to write a fragment of autobiography, a diary of that one year. She began it on her birthday and titled it *Time to Be in Earnest.*

My dictionary defines *earnest* as "serious in intention, not trifling, zealous, intense, ardent, resulting from or displaying conviction." Confronting the brevity of life leads me to solemn and earnest living. When Moses calls me to number my days (see Psalm 90:12), he reminds me that no matter my current age, now is the time to be in earnest. *Father God, in five days, another birthday. Show me what an earnest life looks like.* I look at Jesus and decide that it isn't a frantic and harried life, yet no one lived the definition of earnest better. He was "serious in intention, not trifling, zealous, intense, ardent, resulting from or displaying conviction."

Puritan Thomas Dale wrote regarding wise and earnest living, "It is to take the measure of our days as compared with the work to be performed, with the provision to be laid up for eternity, with the preparation to be made for death, with the precaution to be taken against judgment."[1] I've used Dale's four phrases as a guide as I consider my preparation for Phase 2.

Taking the Measure of My Days in Relation to the Work to Be Performed

"I do not run like someone running aimlessly; I do not fight like a boxer beating the air. No, I strike a blow to my body and make it my slave so that after I have preached to others, I myself will not be disqualified for the prize" (1 Corinthians 9:26-27). Paul used images of the disciplined, high level, competitive athlete to convey—no, declare—his earnest and vigorous commitment to engage fully in God's purposes in the world. As Paul oriented himself to the finish line, he drew on jarring images; he spoke of beating his body and making it his slave. The word picture in the Greek suggests "keeping his flesh under" and "giving [it] a black eye,"[2] which is miles from the practice of self-flagellation or donning the hair shirt. This is not penance; Christ has paid the penalty for sin. Rather, Paul determines that his body will not rule him. He will rule over it. Why this tough stance? Perhaps Paul observed others who meandered and malingered through life without regard to the mission God set before them, shadowboxing, coddling themselves, never earnestly engaging to advance God's kingdom. The word *disqualified* has the sense of not standing the test. The danger is *not* losing salvation but not faithfully finishing the course. Paul intends to run the race all the way to the finish line.

Am I clear on what God has asked me to do? What is the work to be performed? Above all else, God calls me to the work of believing, the work of faith. Jesus said, "The work of God is this: to believe in the one he has sent" (John 6:29). My work is to believe and to help others believe. Before Jesus ascended into heaven, He clarified the mission:

> All authority in heaven and on earth has been given to me.
> Therefore go and make disciples of all nations, baptizing them in

the name of the Father and of the Son and of the Holy Spirit, and teaching them to obey everything I have commanded you. And surely I am with you always, to the very end of the age. (Matthew 28:18-20)

This is my work until I die or He returns.

Oddly, this doesn't stir me to frantic action. Instead, the immensity of the task settles me and entwines me with Jesus. I consider His earnest ministry and observe that He lived amidst needs. Yet Jesus didn't heal everyone. Though He fed multitudes, many remained unfed. Unmet needs did not drain Jesus. The work was not burdensome but nourishing. Jesus said, "My food . . . is to do the will of him who sent me and to finish his work" (John 4:34). The Beloved Son earnestly (and joyfully) finished His work under the Father's eye.

> Today, this week, this year, Lord, what would You have me do? As I look at my life, my days, my day, does it reflect an earnest pursuit to fulfill Your call on my life? In light of Your call, what do I need to say yes to and no to? Father, crystallize my task that I might approach my calling with clarity. Guide and direct my choices that I might not be diverted. Energize me with Your indwelling presence that I might persevere to the end. Bless my labors.

Taking the Measure of My Days in Regard to the Provision I Will Lay Up for Eternity

Soon it will be too late to invest in eternity. Am I exercising faith? Is my hope a growing composition of ever-deepening content? Is Phase 2 increasingly real and relevant, informing and influencing Phase 1 more and more? Does my hope of glory animate my thoughts, determine my values, and invigorate my actions? Am I using my varied resources with Phase 2 in mind?

Some years ago, *Christianity Today* did a series on women from earlier centuries whose lives showed faith, courage, and fortitude. I especially remember Marcella, a woman of great wealth who invested in eternity. She gave her wealth to supply the needs of others in the name of Christ. Later in her life, when robbers came, she had nothing left to give them. She told the robbers in essence, "I sent it all ahead." Marcella died at the hands of the robbers, having used worldly wealth to lay up reward in heaven. Jesus said, "Store up for yourselves treasures in heaven, where moths and rust do not destroy, and where thieves do not break in and steal. For where your treasure is, there your heart will be also" (Matthew 6:20-21).

Years ago, my husband helped me see Phase 2 in a parable (see Luke 16:1-15) that struck me as strange. Jesus tells the story: The manager of a rich man's estate is called on the carpet for mismanagement of his employer's resources. Seeing that he was about to be fired and knowing that he was too old to do manual labor and too proud to beg, the wily manager executed a shrewd plan. He called in those indebted to his master and reduced their debt. He planned to obligate them to welcome him into their homes after he lost his job. Surprisingly, Jesus concluded, "The master commended the dishonest manager because he had acted shrewdly. For the people of this world are more shrewd in dealing with their own kind than are the people of the light. I tell you, use worldly wealth to gain friends for yourselves, so that when it is gone, you will be welcomed into eternal dwellings" (verses 8-9).

I ponder the point of this strange story. Is Jesus calling the "people of the light" to dishonesty? No. But He makes clear that I can use worldly wealth to ensure that friends will be in heaven to welcome me. I can use my resources to give others a chance to hear the gospel. Having neighbors for dinner or supporting missionaries or sponsoring a poor child is an investment in eternity.

Heavenly Father, help me move my best thoughts of You into practical actions. Show me how to use my earthly resources to advance Your kingdom. What would You have me do *now* that will bring others into Your kingdom?

Precaution Against Judgment

"We must all appear before the judgment seat of Christ, so that each of us may receive what is due us for the things done while in the body" (2 Corinthians 5:10). I know that the believer in Jesus Christ will not face judgment for sin. Jesus paid that penalty on the cross. I stand before the Judge covered in the righteousness of Christ. But God will judge my works. Will my labors be burned away into nothingness, or will they stand as testimony to an earnest life (see 1 Corinthians 3:12-15)?

Some say that they are not motivated by this coming judgment. Evidently, Jesus wants us to be or He wouldn't have mentioned it, and He mentioned it more than once. Just as Jesus saves me by grace through faith, He allows me the privilege to colabor with Him by grace through faith. His grace is more than granting undeserved forgiveness and salvation; His grace calls me into His divine and eternal purposes, into colaborship. The believers' judgment and reward is not contrary to grace but rather another exalted expression of it.

Ruminations: My Last Quarter

At sixty-seven, I may not yet have entered the final quarter of my life. All I know is that unless Jesus returns first, I will die. Now is the time to take the measure of my days as compared with the work to be performed, with the provision to be laid up for eternity, with the preparation to be made for death, with the precaution to be taken against judgment.

Suppose I have a quarter of my life ahead of me. What then? The possibility that I might have twenty-five years left is exhilarating. The possibility that I might have *one* more year left is just as exhilarating.

I asked the Lord once, "If I had only one year left to live, what would be my best contribution to the body?" Now I ask, "Lord, if I have a whopping twenty-five years left, what is my best contribution?"

In many sports, the game is won or lost in the final quarter. Nothing is so disheartening to avid fans than to see excellent play for three quarters give way to flabby, lifeless, careless play at the end. The last quarter of play has special challenges. The players are weary, but the end is in sight. Now is the time to be in earnest, whatever my age.

Lord, energize me for the kick at the finish line. When I think about the days remaining, I glory in Your keeping power, Your energizing Spirit, Your very great and precious promises. Keep me. Ignite me to trust and obey to the end. May I stand before You my last day having lived an earnest life.

CHAPTER 31

PREPARING FOR DEATH: STOCKING THE AMMUNITION BOX

I thought: all this is only preparation for learning, at last, how to die.

CZESLAW MILOSZ

My mother saw death coming and cleaned out the attic and basement. She sorted, organized, and tossed. She stashed important papers in a WWII gun-metal-gray ammunition box, ready and available. Whenever I was home, she pulled out the box and took me through the contents. I'm grateful for her thoughtful labors that made everything easier for my brother and me. Her example is a model for me of the preparations I want to make spiritually for my death.

I agree with Dag Hammarskjöld, former president of the United Nations, that "no choice is uninfluenced by the way in which the personality regards its destiny, and the body its death. In the last analysis, it is our conception of death which decides our answers to all the questions that life puts to us . . . hence, too, the necessity of preparing for it."[1]

As I've worked on this book, the value of preparation surfaces again and again. How do I prepare for my death? As I cut loose the extraneous, what content will I pack in my ammunition box?

A friend with a virulent cancer pursued the question "What does it look like to die well?" After months of thought, she came to the conclusion that it looks the same as to *live* well. How we live affects how we die. All of life is a preparation for death. Giving thought to what kind of person I want to become and how I want to face death will shape my life, enriching and enabling me to live more wisely and fully.

The death of Christ changes death forever.

The first item I'll stash in my ammunition box is the title of a very old book. Puritan writer John Owen wrote *The Death of Death in the Death of Christ.*[2] That title reminds me that Jesus defeated death at the cross. The Resurrection is the proof (see 1 Corinthians 15:26,54). God took a physical body to die in my stead and "break the power of him who holds the power of death — that is, the devil — and free those who all their lives were held in slavery by their fear of death" (Hebrews 2:14-15). The apostle Paul wrote of "Christ Jesus, who has destroyed death and has brought life and immortality to light through the gospel" (2 Timothy 1:10). The Lord Jesus hallowed the grave with His death and defanged it with His resurrection. He goes before me. He bore the full sting of death for me. He suffered under the penalty of my sin and rose victorious. He robbed death of its terror and uncertainty. Death is no longer an unknown, shadowy threat stalking me.

Jesus has changed death forever.

When I trusted Jesus as my Savior, I escaped the menacing grip of spiritual death and eternal death. *Spiritual death* is estrangement from God. This is the spirit-deadness everyone lives in until conversion. Unless Jesus comes first, my physical body will die. This death is the last enemy I will face (see 1 Corinthians 15:26). All people face this end that is not the end. Physical death leads not to oblivion but to eternity. After death is Phase 2: heaven or hell. *Eternal death*, eternal separation from God, awaits those who choose separation from Him in life (see Revelation 20:14-15).

Christ's resurrection wins my resurrection.

Shortly after Jesus' resurrection and ascension, the apostle Peter quoted words penned by David roughly one thousand years before. These words were prophetic, looking forward to Jesus' resurrection:

> I saw the Lord always before me.
>> Because he is at my right hand,
>> I will not be shaken.
> Therefore my heart is glad and my tongue rejoices;
>> my body also will rest in hope,
> because you will not abandon me to the realm of the dead,
>> you will not let your holy one see decay.
> You have made known to me the paths of life;
>> you will fill me with joy in your presence. (Acts 2:25-28)

This promise fortified the Son of Man. Jesus knew that death was not the end and that His death and resurrection were the culmination of the earthly race laid out for Him. His death was a portal through which He had to go to receive the promises.

This promise fortifies me, too. I will leave the lid of the ammunition box ajar. I will come here often. I will handle the contents of this passage. I will keep my eyes on Him who has gone ahead in death and resurrection. God will not abandon me to the grave, either. In Jesus, I am on the path of life, where I will live with Him forever.

My times are in His hands.

"All the days ordained for me were written in your book before one of them came to be" (Psalm 139:16). The number of my days and the time and circumstances of my death are not matters of chance. The Craftsman, who tenderly oversaw my beginning, will attend my end (see verses 13-14). "Precious in the sight of the LORD is the death of his faithful servants" (116:15). God of the macro, sustaining all creation by His Word, calling every star by name, notices and holds dear the death of those who belong to Him. God—who created the smallest particles, who holds together the micro, the minute, the nano—notes and finds precious the death of each of His children.

He will be with me.

David faced a mortal threat and sang, "Even though I walk through the darkest valley, I will fear no evil, for you are with me; your rod and your staff, they comfort me" (Psalm 23:4). For You are *with* me. The promise is clear and dear: God will be *with* me in the throes of death, as the cable is severed, as my skiff bobs across the Jordan and bumps onto the shore of heaven. He will be with me in life and in death (see Isaiah 43:2; Hebrews 13:5; Romans 8:37-39). I will fear no evil.

Throughout the Scriptures, God says, "Fear not," and "I will be with you." Obviously, these are the assurances I most need to hear. I hear His promise to be *with* me, but I don't begin to grasp the wonder of it. God Almighty, *with* me. When the great eighteenth-century evangelist John Wesley lay dying, the reality appeared to have swept over him. He rose to consciousness and twice exclaimed, "The best of all is, God is with us."[3]

I am secure in life and death.

I add to the box that Christ reigns in life and is victor over death. I am His and safe in His keeping. He oversees my sojourn (see Philippians 1:6), though I am but a blip on the radar. Whatever shape my death takes, He will keep me. I face my life and death with confidence and expectation: "I eagerly expect and hope that I will in no way be ashamed, but will have sufficient courage so that now as always Christ will be exalted in my body, whether by life or by death. For to me, to live is Christ and to die is gain" (verses 20-21). Paul said that life with Christ is good but that what follows death is better by far, so I approach death knowing, as the archbishop knew in T. S. Eliot's play *Murder in the Cathedral,* that "I am not in danger: only near to death."[4] The archbishop went on to say, "I have had a tremour of bliss, a wink of heaven, a whisper, and I would no longer be denied; all things proceed to a joyful consummation."[5]

Final Preparations

I want to make thoughtful, practical preparations like my mother did: purge possessions, update and organize important papers, make funeral arrangements in advance, keep the house in shape to sell. But, more, I want to make spirit and mind preparations.

Richard Redmer wrote that John Donne died days after delivering his own funeral sermon: "It was preached not many dayes before his death; as if, having done this, there remained nothing for him to doe, but to die."[6] Redmer went on, "May wee make such use of this and other the like preparatives, That neither death, whensoever it shall come, may seeme terrible; nor life tedious, how long soever it shall last."[7]

Perhaps the rest of my life is my funeral sermon. I will deliver it day by day. The rest of my life is my preparation for death—and life forevermore.

Father, I put all this in my ammo box, ready—riches to return to, to unpack, to handle, enlarge, and deepen. Gather me up, Lord, in Your tender care, in Your very great and precious promises, in Your oversight of my life and death and glorious future. And so I sing the last verse of the great hymn "O Sacred Head, Now Wounded."[8]

Be near me when I'm dying,
O, show thy cross to me;
And to my succor flying
Come, Lord, and set me free!
These eyes new faith receiving,
From Jesus shall not move;
For he who dies believing,
Dies safely through thy love.

NOTES

Chapter 2: Why I Wrote This Book, How I Plan to Use It, and How You Might Use It Too

1. Arthur Bennett, ed., *The Valley of Vision: A Collection of Puritan Prayers and Devotions* (Carlisle, PA: Banner of Truth, 1975).
2. Katherine Anne Porter, in George Plimpton, ed., *Women Writers at Work: The Paris Review Interviews*, Second Series (New York: Viking, 1963), 150–151.

Chapter 3: Resolution 52: Commitment to a Reflective Life

1. Jonathan Edwards, *Jonathan Edwards' Resolutions: And Advice to Young Converts*, ed. Stephen J. Nichols (Phillipsburg, NJ: P&R Publishing, 2001).

Chapter 4: A Prepared Life: The Art of Advance-Work Toward an End

1. Regina Sara Ryan, *The Fine Art of Recuperation: A Guide to Surviving and Thriving After Illness, Accident, or Injury* (New York: Tarcher, 1989).
2. Marcus Tullius Cicero, *Letters of Marcus Tullius Cicero with His Treatises on Friendship and Old Age*, Harvard Classics (New York: P. F. Collier & Son, 1937), 9:45.

3. Louis Pasteur, in John Barlett, *Bartlett's Familiar Quotations*, 17th ed. (New York: Little, Brown, 2002), 533.8.

4. Cicero, 47.

5. Katharine Graham, *Vital Speeches of the Day* 61, no. 20 (August 1, 1995).

6. Mark Buchanan, *Spiritual Rhythm: Being with Jesus Every Season of Your Soul* (Grand Rapids, MI: Zondervan, 2010), 150.

Chapter 5: My Intended Wing: Resolving an Inner Conflict

1. Archibald Thomas Robertson, *Word Pictures in the New Testament: Epistles of Paul* (Grand Rapids, MI: Baker, 1931), 4:375.

2. John Milton, *Paradise Lost*, book 9 (London: 1668).

3. Ralph P. Martin, *The Epistle of St. Paul to the Philippians*, Tyndale New Testament Commentaries (London: Tyndale, 1964), 75.

Chapter 7: Teach Us to Number Our Days: The Ministry of the Obituary

1. Don DeLillo, *White Noise* (New York: Penguin Books, 1985), 99.

2. Billy Collins, *Nine Horses* (New York: Random House, 2002), 11.

3. Kay Redfield Jamison, *Exuberance: The Passion for Life* (New York: Vintage Books, 2005), 33–35.

4. Henry Melville, in Charles H. Spurgeon, *The Treasury of David* (Maclean, VA: Macdonald, n.d.), 2:82.

Chapter 9: The Gospel from the Other Side

1. John Henry Jowett, *The Silver Lining* (London: Andrew Melrose, 1919), 202.

Chapter 13: Deep Tracks: A Scaffold of Discipline and Creativity

1. Annie Dillard, *The Writing Life* (New York: Harper & Row, 1989), 32.

Chapter 14: Blessed Imagination: Living a Reverent and Kind Life

1. John Ruskin, in John Henry Jowett, *Brooks by the Traveller's Way* (London: H. R. Allenson, 1902), 124.

2. Percy Bysshe Shelley, *A Defence of Poetry*, Harvard Classics (New York: P. F. Collier & Son, 1937), 27:356.
3. Jowett, 124.
4. Jowett, 125–126.
5. C. H. Spurgeon, *Lectures to My Students* (Grand Rapids, MI: Ministry Resources Library, 1954), 106.

Chapter 15: Like a Little Child
1. Michel Quoist, *Prayers* (New York: Sheed and Ward, 1963), 3.
2. Joseph H. Thayer, *Thayer's Greek-English Lexicon of the New Testament* (Grand Rapids, MI: Baker, 1977), 70.

Chapter 19: Fruitful Every Season
1. G. Campbell Morgan, *The Gospel According to John* (London: Marshall, Morgan & Scott, 1946), 254–255.

Chapter 20: Bee Tree: Investing in Forever
1. Leonardo da Vinci, in John Bartlett, *Bartlett's Familiar Quotations*, 17th ed. (New York: Little, Brown, 2002), 140.3.

Chapter 21: Raised Veins: The Body's Ministry to Me
1. Annie Dillard, *Holy the Firm* (New York: Harper & Row, 1977), 25.

Chapter 22: Wise Reframing: Keeping My Core in Life's Transitions
1. William Wordsworth, *The Sonnet*, Harvard Classics (New York: P. F. Collier & Son, 1937), 41:681.
2. John Milton, *The Complete Poems of John Milton*, Harvard Classics (New York: P. F. Collier & Son, 1937), 4:84.

Chapter 24: Tripped Up: Drink, Drugs, Sex, Materialism, and Other Dangers
1. Rev. F. W. Farrar, *Solomon: His Life and Times* (London: James Nisbet, 1887), 143.
2. Francois Mauriac, in Philip Yancey, *The Jesus I Never Knew* (Grand Rapids, MI: Zondervan, 1995), 118.

Chapter 25: The Lump: When Failure Threatens to Overwhelm

1. James Strong, *Strong's Exhaustive Concordance of the Bible* (Peabody, MA: Hendrickson, 2009), entry 2666.
2. Søren Kierkegaard, in Martin E. Marty, *Context: A Commentary on the Interaction of Religion and Culture* (Claretian, 1968), 4.

Chapter 26: Embracing the Cross: Preparing to Drink My Cup

1. J. D. Douglas, ed., *New Bible Dictionary* (London: InterVarsity, 1962), 283.
2. See also Isaiah 51:17; Ezekiel 23:32-34; Habakkuk 2:16.
3. Alexander Maclaren, in J. Oswald Sanders, *The Incomparable Christ* (Chicago: Moody, 1971), 204.

Chapter 29: Widowhood: What Shape Will My New Life Take?

1. Kay Redfield Jamison, *Nothing Was the Same* (New York: Knopf, 2009), 182.
2. Jamison, 185.

Chapter 30: Time to Be in Earnest

1. Thomas Dale, in C. H. Spurgeon, *The Treasury of David* (McLean, VA: MacDonald, n.d.), 2:81.
2. M. R. Vincent, *Word Studies in the New Testament* (MacDill Air Force Base, FL: MacDonald Publishing Company, n.d.), 781.

Chapter 31: Preparing for Death: Stocking the Ammunition Box

1. Dag Hammarskjöld, in Karlis Osis, PhD, and Erlendur Haraldsson, PhD, *At the Hour of Death* (Norwalk, CT: Hastings House, 1977), 1.
2. John Owen, *The Death of Death in the Death of Christ: A Treatise in Which the Whole Controversy About Universal Redemption Is Fully Discussed* (London: Banner of Truth, 1959).
3. J. C. Ryle, *Christian Leaders of the 18th Century* (Carlisle, PA: Banner of Truth, 1978), 81.
4. T. S. Eliot, *Murder in the Cathedral* (New York: Harcourt, 1963), 70.

5. Eliot, 70.
6. Richard Redmer, *The Complete Poetry and Selected Prose of John Donne* (New York: Random House, 1994), 576.
7. Redmer, 576.
8. Paul Gerhardt, "O Sacred Head, Now Wounded," trans. J. W. Alexander, http://www.bartleby.com/270/11/48.html.

ABOUT THE AUTHOR

JEAN FLEMING grew up in Maryland, came to Christ in her senior year of high school, and met a Navigator-trained fellow student in college. She married Roger in 1965 and they went to their first staff assignment with The Navigators in San Diego, California, followed by assignments to South Korea, Okinawa, Tucson, Seattle, Colorado Springs, and Montrose, Colorado.

Jean's primary ministry focus has been one-to-one ministry with a passion to touch the generations behind her for the future of the work of Christ. She has also written *A Mother's Heart*, *Between Walden and the Whirlwind* (reprinted as *Finding Focus in a Whirlwind World*), *Homesick Heart*, *Feeding Your Soul*, and magazine articles.

More by Jean Fleming.

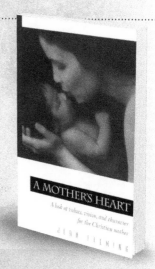

NAV ESSENTIALS

Voices of The Navigators—Past, Present, and Future

NavEssentials offer core Navigator messages from such authors as Jim Downing, LeRoy Eims, Mike Treneer, and more — at an affordable price. This new series will deeply influence generations in the movement of discipleship. Learn from the old and new messages of The Navigators how powerful and transformational the life of a disciple truly is.

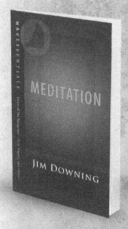

Meditation
by Jim Downing
9781615217250 | $5.00

Advancing the Gospel
by Mike Treneer
9781617471575 | $5.00

The Triumph of Surrender
by William M. Fletcher
9781615219070 | $4.99

Available wherever books are sold. NAVPRESS